Kneeling We Triumph

Volume One

By the same Authors

The Amazing Book Vols. 1 & 2
Asking Father
The "Call Back" Series
The Christian's Daily Challenge
Covetousness
Father Calling
Him or It
The "How They Prayed" Series
The King's Diamond
Let My People Go
The New Creation
The "Royal" Series
Soul Sculpture
The "They Knew Their God" Series
To Judge or Not To Judge?

Kneeling We Triumph

Volume One

Compiled by

Edwin and Lillian Harvey

BRITISH ADDRESS

Harvey Christian Publishers UK

P.O. Box 510, Cheadle

Stoke-on-Trent, ST10 2NQ

Tel./Fax (01538) 752291

E-mail: jjcook@mac.com

UNITED STATES ADDRESS

Harvey Christian Publishers, Inc.

3107 Hwy. 321, Hampton, TN 37658

Tel./Fax (423) 768-2297

E-mail: books@harveycp.com

http://www.harveycp.com

Acknowledgments

In seeking to obtain permission to use copyright material, we have met with a most courteous and kindly response from both publishers and authors. We take this occasion to express our thanks in the following instances: A. & C. Black for an extract from the poem "Art and Heart" by Ella Wheeler Wilcox; The Allahabad Bible Seminary (O.M.S.) for the selection by Dr. Wesley Duewel from *Revival* magazine; Rev. Stanley Banks for quotations by himself and Mr. J. D. Drysdale; Mr. George E. Failing for selections from his own writings; God's Revivalist Press for the quotation by G. D. Watson; The Editor, *The Alliance Witness*, for excerpts by Dr. A. W. Tozer and Dr. A. B. Simpson; Peter Davies Ltd. for extracts by Mrs. Catherine Marshall from her books, *A Man Called* Peter and *To Live Again*; Mrs. Jean L. Gee for the quotation by her late husband, Donald Gee; Rev. Armin R. Gesswein for quotations from his own writings; Mrs. V. Hood for the poem by Edith Hickman Divall; Messrs. Hodder & Stoughton Ltd. for the selections by Samuel Chadwick and G. Campbell Morgan; Lutterworth Press for the quotations by Frank Laubach; Macmillan of London and Basingstoke for the selections by Sadhu Sundar Singh from the book, *The Sadhu*, by Streeter and Appasamy; Marshall, Morgan & Scott Ltd. for quotations by F. J. Huegel from his books, *Bone of His Bone* and *The Cross of Christ—The Throne of God*, and the quotations by Gordon B. Watt from his book, *Effectual Fervent Praying*; Overseas Missionary Fellowship for selections by J. O. Fraser, D. E. Hoste, Mrs. Howard Taylor, and Leslie Lyall; Mrs. Alice Hansche Mortenson for her poem, "Let Me Listen"; The Paternoster Press for the quotation by G. H. Lang; Pickering & Inglis Ltd. for the poem, "If We Could Only Be Still," by Edith Hickman Divall; Mr. Leonard Ravenhill for the extracts from his book, *Why*

Revival Tarries, and for the selection by W. Mallis from *Dayspring*; Dr. Alan Redpath for the extract from his writings; Fleming H. Revell Co. for the quotations by S. D. Gordon from his book, *Quiet Talks on Prayer*; The Salvation Army for quotations by Samuel Logan Brengle; S. P. C. K. for the selections by Lilias Trotter from the book, *The Master of The Impossible*, edited by Constance E. Padwick, and for the quotation by Amy Wilson Carmichael from her biography, *Amy Carmichael of Dohnavur*, by Frank Houghton, and the extract by Thomas Walker from *Walker of Tinnevelly* by Amy Wilson Carmichael; Victory Press for the quotation by Watchman Nee from the book, *Love Not The World*; Mrs. Ruth L. H. Wigglesworth for the poem by her late father, E. C. W. Boulton.

Many of the poems, quotations, and extracts used in the book have been gleaned over a period of years from such varied sources that in numbers of cases it has been impossible, after considerable effort, to trace either the publisher or the author. Where omissions have been made and due credit has not been given, we beg indulgence.

Foreword

Like many other Christian workers who have been anxious to be successful in labor for God we have been forced to the conclusion that the Holy Spirit alone can effect lasting results. During these past years of heart-searching study, we have gathered together similar conclusions from many God-honored ministers and missionaries who have discovered the secret that the Holy Spirit comes to our aid when, wearied with self-effort, we ask, seek, and knock. We long very much to share with God's children some of these readings and to spread them as widely as possible. We ask humbly that the lives and labors of many who read will be revived and blessed by the pages of *Kneeling We Triumph* in Volumes I and II.

Each book contains sixty readings on prayer which are a storehouse of precious nuggets on the subject. We have arranged them in what seems to us logical catagories such as "Importance of Prayer," "Time for Prayer," "Prayer and Communion," "Hindrances to Prayer," "Persevering Prayer," "Intercessory Prayer," and "Prayer and Faith."

We express our indebtedness to our many friends and prayer-partners who have so encouraged us in this work. We especially thank our fellow-workers who have so unstintingly aided in proof-reading, typing, and in many other ways. We now send forth *Kneeling We Triumph* with the earnest prayer that the message will help toward a reviving of prayer on all fronts.

Edwin and Lillian Harvey,
Lancashire, England, 1971.

Prayer
is God's Method

I will therefore that men pray every where, lifting up holy hands (1 Tim. 2:8).

Men ought always to pray (Luke 18:1).

Praying always with all prayer (Eph. 6:18).

Prayer is not our message; it is the method of God for the message. Everything is by prayer. I did not even read the Book of Acts in seminary. I had always considered it a historical document. When I got into it later, it was a brand new book to me. I discovered that the method of the Spirit of God in that book was a prayer method, and I started praying for a spiritual awakening.

About that time I began to read everything I could find by Charles G. Finney. I discovered that his revivals were based on prayer, that the spirit of prayer is the spirit of revival. Then I met an old Methodist lay preacher and through him I learned that in the early American revivals they used to major in prayer—nights of prayer, all kinds of prayer. The evangelists would preach on the subject. And as in the Book of Acts, they "continued steadfastly in the apostles' doctrine and fellowship, and in breaking of bread, and in prayers."

So I came to have a kind of vision of prayer—not a picture vision, but an inward vision. I sensed that if God is going to do it, it has to be by prayer. Prayer is not just a good idea—it is His divine plan. . . .

Our generation has yet to see prayer as a ministry, and to take God at His Word on this subject. It is **while** we pray that God works, if we can but see Him—not merely before, or after prayer. Our idea is, "Let us pray, and then get on with the work." But prayer is our real work. We so often think of prayer as a prefix or a suffix to an otherwise busy round. But God's works are wrought **as** we pray, and **while** we pray.

It brings a revolution to any minister or Christian, once he believes God's Word on this point. His works are done through prayer, for He

8

always works out from His throne by intercession. It is not only His intercession, but ours too, for, by His Spirit, He not only prays for us, but in us. He gives us of His own great praying—and that is true praying indeed.

We are not just to imitate His praying, but to enter into it, receive it, and have it enter into us. That is how we enter into His works, become "laborers together with God," and learn to cease from our own works. We learn in this way to work **with** Him, instead of **for** Him. Sons, and no longer slaves.

Then after we have prayed, we walk with the Lord Jesus into the works He has wrought in answer to prayer. Prayer is our real work. Working is drudgery. Even working **for** the Lord is dreary. But working **with** Him is delight. In His Kingdom, it is those to whom He ministers who minister. The conquered conquer, and the followers of Christ lead others.—Armin Gesswein.

God does nothing but by prayer, and everything with it.
—John Wesley.

Every great movement of God can be traced to a kneeling figure.
—D. L. Moody.

The Young Men's Christian Association can be traced to the kneeling figure of a very young man, George Williams, who believed that by prayer he could influence his companions in the large draper's establishment where he worked. Conditions among the young employees were dreadful, but he won them one by one and this is his own account of how he went about it: "The Lord having closed me in, I was enabled to plead, and I believe the Lord has given me . . ." (three names of assistants in the same business). "O Lord, now come down and let me plead with Thee until I prevail." At the end of the year there were nine, and in a few brief years the whole establishment had felt the impact of this young man from the country who dared defy the wickedness in London, and claimed for Christ those whom Satan had captured.

The Greater Work

Greater works than these shall he do; because I go unto my Father. And whatsoever ye shall ask in my name, that will I do (John 14:12,13).

There is no way that Christians, in a private capacity, can do so much to promote the work of God and advance the kingdom of Christ as by prayer.—Jonathan Edwards.

Prayer is releasing the energies of God. For prayer is asking God to do what we cannot do.—Charles Trumbull.

Prayer does not fit us for the greater works; prayer is the greater work. We think of prayer as a common-sense exercise of our higher powers in order to prepare us for God's work. In the teaching of Jesus Christ prayer is the working of the miracle of Redemption in me which produces the miracle of Redemption in others by the power of God. . . . Prayer is the battle; it is a matter of indifference where you are. Whichever way God engineers circumstances, the duty is to pray. Never allow the thought, "I am of no use where I am," because you certainly can be of no use where you are not. Wherever God has dumped you down in circumstances, pray, ejaculate to Him all the time. "Whatsoever ye ask in My name, that will I do." We won't pray unless we get thrills; that is the intensest form of spiritual selfishness. We have to labor along the line of God's direction, and He says **pray.** "Pray ye therefore the Lord of the harvest, that he will send forth laborers into his harvest. . . ."

The great enemy to the Lord Jesus Christ in the present day is the conception of practical work that has not come from the New Testament, but from the systems of the world in which endless energy and activities are insisted upon, but no private life with God. The emphasis is put on the wrong thing. Jesus said, "The kingdom of God cometh not with observation . . . for, behold, the kingdom of God is within you," a hidden, obscure thing. An active Christian worker too often lives in the shop window. It is the innermost of the innermost that reveals the power of the life.

We have to get rid of the plague of the spirit of the religious age in which we live. In our Lord's life there was none of the press and rush of tremendous activity that we regard so highly, and the disciple is to be as his Master. The central thing about the kingdom of Jesus Christ is a personal relationship to Himself, not public usefulness to men.—Oswald Chambers.

Of "Praying Hyde" and his preparation for a convention in India his biographer says: "It was determined that prayer and not preaching should be recognized as the great channel of blessing. To this end a prayer-room was established as the Power House of the movement. Here, before the Convention began, Hyde and his friends spent thirty days and thirty nights in prayer, and throughout the ten days of the Convention, Hyde really lived here.

"He spent most of the time on his face, for he felt he never could get low enough before God, pausing sometimes to take a little food and at times throwing himself down in a corner for a little sleep. He shunned publicity, but when he did speak, though his utterance was quiet, his words had a burning power. In the prayer-room he obtained the Tongue of Fire."

Mr. Philips, biographer of Whitefield, wrote: "After all, the grand secret of Whitefield's power was his devotional spirit. Had he been less prayerful, he would have been less powerful. He was the prince of preachers without the veil, because he was a Jacob within the veil. His face shone when he came down from the mount, because he had been long alone with God upon the mount. It was this which won for him the title seraphic, not in the scholastic, but in the angelic sense of the term."

Prayer—
the Moving Ministry

And when they had prayed, the place was shaken where they were assembled together . . . and with great power gave the apostles witness . . . and great grace was upon them all (Acts 4:31, 33).

At midnight Paul and Silas prayed, and sang. . . . And suddenly there was a great earthquake (Acts 16:25, 26).

Speaking of travailing in prayer through the Spirit, that noble and good woman, Mrs. Catherine Booth, had this to say to younger converts:

"It was one of the things in which I grieved the Spirit of God in my early days, that I would not let Him, to the extent He would have done, make me a woman of prayer; and yet, in comparison with many, perhaps, I was one. He used to lay particular people and subjects on my heart, so that I could not help praying; but, oh! how bitterly I have regretted and wept before the Lord that I did not let Him have all His way with me in this respect.

"Take warning! and you whom He is beginning to lead, let Him lead you. Pour out your souls for others and with others. I believe that more souls are convinced in real prayer than in speaking. I have noticed this many a time. I have seen at the bottom of a great hall or theatre, or in the gallery, a lot of the roughest men conceivable, behaving in the most unseemly manner, arrested by the influence of prayer. Perhaps, when the rowdyism has been ready to break into open tumult, a little woman has stretched out her hands over the congregation, and said, 'Now, let us pray,' and I have seen the whole mass of men assume an attitude of quietness and reverence. I have watched the aspect of the congregation, and have seen great, rough, black-faced fellows get their heads down, and sometimes wipe their eyes; and when we have got up to sing, there has been no more disorderly conduct, but they have settled down with the solemnity of death to listen. Hundreds of them were convinced of sin while under that prayer. It was the Holy

Ghost wrestling for those souls in the heart of that woman that struck them with conviction.

"Prayer is agony of soul—wrestling of the spirit. You know how men and women deal with one another when they are in desperate earnestness for something to be done. That is prayer, whether it be to man or God; and when you get your heart influenced, and melted, and wrought up, and burdened by the Holy Ghost for souls, you will have power, and you will never pray but somebody will be convinced— some poor soul's dark eyes will be opened, and spiritual life will commence."

> From strength to strength go on,
> Wrestle, and fight, and pray,
> Tread all the powers of darkness down,
> And win the well-fought day;
> Still let the Spirit cry
> In all His soldiers: Come!
> Till Christ the Lord descend from high,
> And take the conquerors home.
> —Charles Wesley.

The direct power of prayer is, in a sense, omnipotent. Prayer moves the hand that moves the world. It secures for the believer the resources of divinity. What battles has it not fought! What victories has it not won! What burdens has it not carried! What wounds has it not healed! What griefs has it not assuaged! It is the wealth of poverty, the refuge of affliction, the strength of weakness, the light of darkness. It is the oratory that gives power to the pulpit. It is the hand that strikes down Satan and breaks the fetters of sin. It turns the scales of fate more than the edge of the sword, the craft of the statesmen, or the weight of scepters. It has arrested the wings of time, turned aside the very scythe of death, and discharged Heaven's frowning and darkest cloud in a shower of blessings.—Guthrie.

Prayer
is Omnipotent

Thou that hearest prayer, unto thee shall all flesh come (Psa. 65:2).

Thus saith the LORD God of Israel, That which thou hast prayed to me . . . I have heard (2 Kings 19:20).

The devil is not afraid of machinery; he is only afraid of God, and machinery without prayer is machinery without God. Our day is characterized by the multiplication of man's machinery and the diminution of God's power sought and obtained by prayer. But when men and women arise who believe in prayer, and who pray in the way the Bible teaches us to pray, prayer accomplishes as much as it ever did. Prayer can do today as much as it ever could. Prayer can do anything God can do, for the arm of God responds to the touch of prayer. All the infinite resources of God are at the command of prayer. Prayer is the key that opens wide the inexhaustible storehouses of divine grace and power. "Ask, and it shall be given you," cries our Heavenly Father, as He swings wide open the doors of the divine treasure-house. There is only one limit to what prayer can do; that is what God can do. But all things are possible to God; therefore prayer is omnipotent.

Christian history and Christian biography demonstrate the truth of what the Word of God teaches about prayer. All through the history of the Church, men and women have arisen in all ranks of life who believed with simple, child-like faith what the Bible teaches about prayer and they have asked and they have received. But what are some of the definite things that prayer has power to do?

There is mighty power in prayer. It has much to do with our obtaining fullness of power in Christian life and service. The one who will not take time for prayer may as well resign all hope of obtaining the fullness of power God has for him. It is "they that wait upon the

Lord" who "shall renew their strength" (Isa.40:31). Waiting upon the Lord means something more than spending a few minutes at the beginning and close of each day running through some stereotyped form of request. **"Wait upon the Lord."** True prayer takes time and thought, but it is the great time-saver. At all events if we are to know fullness of power we must be men and women of prayer.—Torrey.

Too oft, when faithless doubtings
     Around our spirits press,
We cry, "Can hands so feeble
     Grasp such Almightiness?"
While thus we doubt and tremble
     Our hold still looser grows;
While on our darkness gazing
     Vainly Thy radiance glows.

Oh, cheer us with Thy brightness,
     And guide us by Thy hand,
In Thy light teach us light to see,
     In Thy strength strong to stand.
Then though our hands be feeble,
     If they but touch Thine arm,
Thy light and power shall lead us
     And keep us strong and calm.
                         —Unknown.

Out of a very intimate acquaintance with D. L. Moody, I wish to testify that he was a far greater pray-er than he was preacher. Time and time again, he was confronted by obstacles that seemed insurmountable, but he always knew the way to surmount and to overcome all difficulties. He knew the way to bring to pass anything that needed to be brought to pass. He knew and believed in the deepest depths of his soul that "nothing was too hard for the Lord" and that prayer could do anything that God could do.—Torrey.

Gateway
to God

Then began men to call upon the name of the LORD (Gen. 4:26).

For the eyes of the Lord are over the righteous, and his ears are open unto their prayers: but the face of the Lord is against them that do evil (1 Peter 3:12).

Prayer is the Christian's greatest resource and the one least used. It is his greatest obligation and the one most neglected. It is the most common form of devotion, yet the one least understood. Prayer is the gateway to God's presence, but few enter. Prayer is the channel of God's grace, but in most lives it is clogged. It is commonly supposed that anyone can pray, but only those who are accepted in Christ have full access to God. Many regard prayer as optional, but God requires prayer as the condition of His working and where there is no prayer, there is no power.—Slocum.

A prominent Christian leader, acquainted with spiritual conditions said: "If I were to put my finger on the greatest lack in our Christianity, I would unhesitantly point to the need for an effective prayer life among laity and ministers." And E. M. Bounds warns us that past praying cannot suffice for today's needs: "The Church that is dependent on its past history for its miracles of power and grace is a fallen Church."

Speaking of Hudson Taylor, D. E. Hoste says: "He was of necessity a busy man, but he always regarded prayer itself as in reality the most needful and important part of the work. He practically recognized that much time must be spent in seeking God's guidance if a right understanding was to be obtained of the problems and difficulties that confronted him, in carrying on the work of the Mission. He knew that in no other way was the power of the Holy Spirit to be obtained for himself and his brethren, as they sought to develop the

16

work. I venture on this occasion not only to impress upon myself but upon you as well the importance of our copying him in this respect."

And Mrs. Howard Taylor, in her biography of Hudson Taylor, quotes him as saying: "Am hoping to give special time to prayer and Bible study on the voyage. I do want our whole life to be an ascending plane—not resting in anything we have learned or felt or attained, but a pressing on and up. . . . Do we not want more really to meditate on God, to gaze on Him, to take in what we are even now competent to take in of His greatness, His resources, His assurances and promises? Dwelling thus on Him, should we not be enabled to grasp more of the heights and depths of His character and purposes and be more ready and able to do His will?"

One of the Lammermuir party, writing home to England, said: "Oh! that we may be made capable of bearing much blessing. Do pray that we may each be drawn close to the Savior, and kept walking with Him in such sweet fellowship that for us to live may be Christ. Then, what wonders should we see! . . . The destitution in the light of eternity is awful. It stares us in the face. Human effort cannot meet it; nothing can, short of divine power. So do pray. Oh, we need to lay hold upon God about it. May He make us really in earnest. How can we trifle, how can we be listless in view of His unfailing promise that what we ask in faith we shall receive? . . . Why are we not Israels? God grant that we may learn how to pray."

Prayer power is not only the most direct, but also the most effective force that can be brought to bear upon the many difficult problems that exist in the Lord's work. Prayer is not only more effective than other methods of carrying forward the work of the Lord, but it has also the further great advantage of being free from human schemes and carnal manipulations.

He who waits upon God, moves on in quiet confidence and needs neither the blare of trumpets nor press agents' methods to announce his success, but in godly fear, leaves until the day of Christ's return the record of achievement. The whole tendency in the life of prayer is to bring us to the place of crucifixion, and to school us in the great principles of righteousness, justice, and love.—Unknown.

Arousing Men to Pray

And I sought for a man among them, that should make up hedge, and stand in the gap before me for the land, that I should not destroy it: but I found none (Ezek. 22:30).

To arouse one man or woman to the tremendous power of prayer for others is worth more than the combined activity of a score of average Christians. What David Brainerd did others may do. God is no respecter of persons.—A. J. Gordon.

E. M. Bounds left his settled pastorate to stir ministers to the importance of prayer. W. H. Hodge here gives a personal glimpse into this intercessor's importunity on behalf of himself and others: "I have been among many ministers and slept in the same room with them for several years. No smoking among them, no secret orders, no jokes, they were beautiful, clean, and good. They prayed, but I was never impressed with any special praying among them until one day a small man with grey hair and an eye like an eagle came along. His stature and little handbag were against him. . . .

"We had a ten-day convention. We had some fine preachers around the home, and he and one of them were assigned to my room. I was surprised early next morning to see a man bathing and rubbing himself before day and then see him get down and begin to pray.

"I said to myself, 'He will not disturb us, but will soon finish.' He kept on softly for hours, interceding and weeping softly, for me and my indifference, and for all the ministers of God.

"He spoke the next day on 'Prayer.' I became interested, for I was young in the ministry, and had often desired to meet with a man of God that prayed like the saints of the apostolic age. Next morning he was up, praying again, and for ten days he was up early, praying for hours. I became intensely interested and thanked God for sending him. 'At last,' I said, 'I have found a man that really prays. I shall never let him go.'

"He drew me to him with hooks of steel; I entertained him, rose up with him, brought him to New York City at quite a cost of money to have him pray for my people and for me. He was a great admirer of David Brainerd. He would read his diary for hours and try to impress his life on others.

"He remained two months with me in sweet fellowship and mighty prevailing prayer. On the 24th day of October, I took that dear, sweet, wrinkled face in my hands, and kissed him for the last time. That face lit up with the divinity of thought, those eyes gazing and peering into immensity—an eagle man, an intense man—yes, one of God's eagles. I shall never see him again in this world; nor the like of him, I fear.

"What a vast difference in this man of God and the ministers of today. They know no battles with the powers of darkness; they know no wrestling with the mighty forces of the air; no hours of travail when the crush of battle looks as though Satan would win (Isa. 66:8, Isa. 64:7).

"Many a minister has buried his spirituality in the grave of his activities. Eight years ago I commenced to pray early. This early rising is no longer an experiment. It is with me a success.

"E. M. Bounds waited fifty years for two men—only two adopted his early praying, one minister and one layman."

Blessed is the day whose morning is sanctified. Successful is the day whose first victory was won by prayer. Holy is the day whose dawn finds thee on the top of the mount! Health is established in the morning. Wealth is won in the morning. The light is brightest in the morning. "Wake, psaltery and harp; I myself will awake early."

—Joseph Parker.

Train Others to Pray

One of his disciples said unto him, Lord, teach us to pray, as John also taught his disciples (Luke 11:1).

The plea and purpose of the apostles were to put the church to praying. They did not ignore the grace of cheerful giving. They were not ignorant of the place which religious activity and work occupied in the spiritual life. But not one or all of these, in apostolic estimate or urgency, could at all compare in necessity and importance with prayer. The most sacred and urgent pleas were used, the most fervid exhortations, the most comprehensive and arousing words were uttered to enforce the all-important obligation and necessity of prayer.

—E. M. Bounds.

In traveling among the nations, John R. Mott made it a practice to study the sources of the spiritual movements which transformed whole communities. Invariably, when he could reach the source, he found it to be intercessory prayer.

"I heard of a man," he says, "who spent three hours a day in intercession."

When someone asked him, "How can we multiply intercessions?" he said, "I used to lay down a great many points on how to get people to pray, but I have made up my mind that the only way to get them is to do it myself."—Selected.

Leaders of men and movements have seen this importance of prayer-training. D. E. Hoste, successor to Hudson Taylor, places this need above all other branches of instruction:

"In connection with the Training Home, the thought sometimes comes to me, in view of the growing emphasis on prayer and intercession in those parts of the field where there has been special spiritual blessing, whether the exercise of them should not have a more definite and larger place in the course of preparation. The leadership would need to be by someone who through much exercise and even travail, has himself been baptized with a true and fervent spirit of prayer.

"Should it not be recognized that the practice of prayer and intercession needs to be taught to young believers, or rather developed in young believers, quite as much, if not more so than other branches of the curriculum?"

The late J. D. Drysdale, founder of Emmanuel Missions and Training School, possessed this same vision:

"If I am concerned that my flock be men and women of prayer, then, as their pastor, I must lead the way; apathy in me will produce apathy in them. The church prayer-meeting ought to be the best attended in the week, and if it is, success will follow the ministry of the Word at the weekends. I would rather a thousand times set men and women to pray than teach them to preach. The homiletical class can teach them to preach."

J. H. Jowett, a most godly and moving preacher, emphasized the same need: "I would rather teach one man to pray than ten men to preach."

In his autobiography, *Bristol Fashion*, Hugh Redwood states that as a young convert no-one had taken the pains to teach him how to pray, and to this he attributed his failing to make the most of a period in his life which could have proved so useful. After years, he rediscovered Christ through prayer. What books we might have had from the pen of this journalist had some simple Christian introduced him to access to God by prayer!

"More ships!" some cry; "More guns! More fighters in the air!"
But wise the King who calls for—more prayer!
Remember, angels use this ancient thoroughfare—
So keep the highways clear: more prayer!
One day will not suffice to meet time's wear and tear;
Each hour of life must see—more prayer!
Again, and yet again, the scrolls of God declare,
The deepest need of men—more prayer!
                                                              —Unknown.

Man's Strange Reluctance to Commune

Adam and his wife hid themselves from the presence of the LORD God (Gen. 3:8).

The LORD looked down from heaven upon the children of men, to see if there were any that did understand, and seek God. They are all gone aside (Psa. 14:2, 3).

If prayer is so marvelous a privilege, why is man so loath to enter into his rich heritage? The observation of this reluctance has puzzled many believers. The answer can only be found in the story of Adam's lost communion in the garden. Disobedience brought departure; obedience means communion. The Old Adam, the flesh, does not delight in God. In the following quotation, A. W. Tozer makes it clear that it is only the enthroned Spirit within the believer Who can enjoy fellowshipping with the Father:

"That first picture of God and man at the time of the creation shows them in close and open-hearted communion. Adam listens while God explains how it is to be with him in his Eden home and lays down a few easy rules for his life on earth. The whole scene is restful, relaxed, and altogether beautiful.

"But the communion did not last. Adam's very likeness to God, viz., his freedom to choose, permitted him, though it did not compel him, to make a choice contrary to the will of God. So sin entered and the wondrous fellowship was broken.

"Seen from our human standpoint, redemption must rank first among all the acts of God. No other achievement of the Godhead required such vast and precise knowledge, such perfection of wisdom, or such fullness of moral power. To bring man into communion with Himself God must deal effectively with the whole matter of justice and righteousness; He must dispose of sin, reconcile an enemy, and make a rebel willingly obedient. And this He must do without compromising His holiness or coercing the race He would save.

22

"How two wills set in opposition to each other, and both free, could be harmonized was God's problem and His alone; and with infinite wisdom and power He solved it through the redemptive work of Jesus Christ our Lord. Because Christ is God and man He can properly represent each before the other. He is the Daysman Who can stand between the alienated man and the offended God and lay His hand upon them both. 'For there is one God, and one mediator between God and men, the man Christ Jesus' (I Tim. 2:5).

"All this is such a familiar part of evangelical theology that it may safely be assumed that the majority of my readers know it already. That is, they know it theoretically, but the experiential aspect of the truth is not so well-known. Indeed large numbers of supposedly sound Christian believers know nothing at all about personal communion with God; and there lies one of the greatest weaknesses of present-day Christianity.

"The experiential knowledge of God is eternal life (John 17:3), and increased knowledge results in a correspondingly larger and fuller life. So rich a treasure is this inward knowledge of God that every other treasure is as nothing compared with it. We may count all things of no value and sacrifice them freely if we may thereby gain a more perfect knowledge of God through Jesus Christ our Lord. This was Paul's testimony (Phil. 3:7-14), and it has been the testimony of all great Christian souls who have followed Christ from Paul's day to ours.

"To know God it is necessary that we be like God to some degree, for things wholly dissimilar cannot agree and beings wholly unlike can never have communion with each other. It is necessary therefore that we use every means of grace to bring our souls into harmony with the character of God."*

*Excerpted from "The Increasing Knowledge of God," in *That Incredible Christian*, by A. W. Tozer. Christian Publications, Inc., Harrisburg, Pa. 1964. Used by permission.

Prayer's Requisite— Co-Crucifixion

If ye abide in me, and my words abide in you, ye shall ask what ye will, and it shall be done unto you (John 15:7).

LORD, who shall abide in thy tabernacle? who shall dwell in thy holy hill? He that walketh uprightly, and worketh righteousness, and speaketh the truth in his heart (Psa. 15:1, 2).

F. J. Huegel was a chaplain in World War I and later served as a missionary in Mexico City. He says of his earlier ministry: "There were years of earnest toil and some little fruit, but in my secret soul I wept in shame for there was a great lack. I was not victorious. I was the victim of a thousand things I loathed."

God permitted him to pass through a very great trial during which he made the discovery that there were demon forces governing the world of which he had never before dreamed, and in the "face of which his weapons were as a toy against a battleship." He learned that his self-life made room for these forces within himself and neutralized his attack against them. And then it dawned upon him as a wonderful reality that God had nailed his old self-life to the Savior's cross centuries before. Little wonder that the words below burn with reality as he urges co-crucifixion with Christ as a condition for authoritative prayer:

"The reason why many are finding prayer so unsatisfactory and the life of prayer so unattractive is because they have attempted to enter into the celestial realms of prayer in the strength of the 'old-man.' The 'old-man' can no more wield these weapons which 'are not carnal but mighty through God,' than he can 'love his enemies,' or 'rejoice always,' or 'have the mind which was in Christ Jesus,' or fulfill any other Christian grace. He (the old-man) may imitate these graces, but actually possess them, never. They are 'the fruits of the Spirit.' They come from above. They are the out-workings of the

Christ-nature imparted to the believer and incorporated in his being on the basis of the Cross.

"True prayer can only be inaugurated on the basis of 'co-crucifixion.' This is the prime condition: 'If ye abide in Me and I in you, ye shall ask whatsoever ye will and it shall be done unto you.' We must be 'in Christ.' But we cannot be in Christ in the fullest sense, without that we commit to death, in the power of the Savior's death, the 'old-life.'

"It is when we realize our oneness with Christ in death and in resurrection, that prayer becomes the marvelous force that we find it was in the life of the Savior, the invincible dynamic that it reveals itself to be in the book of Acts, and the ineffable experience of the great saints of the ages. It is then that our spirits, liberated by the power of the Cross from the fleshly and the soulish entanglements, 'mount up on wings as eagles.' It is then that communion with the infinitely adorable One Who inhabiteth Eternity comes spontaneously and naturally to its fullest expression. It is then that the injunction, 'Pray without ceasing,' ceases to be an unintelligible command; for the spirit released from the thralldom of the 'flesh-life,' and freed from all Satanic oppression by an appropriation of the full benefits of the Calvary victory, rises to take its place with Christ in the Heavenlies where prayer is the continuous in-breathing of the life of God. It is then that prayer, energized by the Spirit of the living God, which it cannot be until it is freed from all selfish ingredients, becomes at times a groaning which is unutterable, and which does not fail to move mountains, and achieve the impossible. It is then that prayer becomes a working out of the will of God, and therefore, must prevail, be the difficulties what they may, however staggering the problem, however great the need. It is then that the great disparity between what the Master said that prayer would accomplish, and the miserable caricature that it is in the actual practice of millions is removed, and prayer blossoms out in all the glory of its true nature."

The Flesh—
Arch-Enemy to Prayer

They that are in the flesh cannot please God (Rom. 8:8).

No flesh should glory in his presence (1 Cor. 1:29).

A life lived according to the flesh, and not according to the Spirit—it is in this that we find the origin of the prayerlessness of which we complain. A brother once said to me: "That is the whole difficulty; we wish to pray in the Spirit, and at the same time walk after the flesh, and this is impossible." . . .

Adam was created to have fellowship with God, and enjoyed it before his Fall. After the Fall, however, there came immediately, a deep-seated aversion to God, and he fled from Him. This incurable aversion is the characteristic of the unregenerate nature, and the chief cause of our unwillingness to surrender ourselves to fellowship with God in prayer. . . .

Scripture teaches us that there are but two conditions possible for the Christian. One is a walk according to the Spirit, the other a walk according to "the flesh." Paul writes to the Galatians: "Are ye so foolish? having begun in the Spirit, are ye now made perfect by the flesh?" (Gal. 3:3). Their service lay in fleshly outward performances. They did not understand that where "the flesh" is permitted to influence their service of God, it soon results in open sin. . . .

There is no means of dealing with "the flesh," save as Christ dealt with it, bearing it to the cross. "Our old man is crucified with him" (Rom. 6:6), so we by faith also crucify it, and regard and treat it daily as an accursed thing that finds its rightful place on the accursed cross. . . . Would that we might understand God's counsels of grace for us! "The flesh" on the cross—the Spirit in the heart and controlling the life!

Here then we have the deep root of evil as the cause of a prayerless life. "The flesh" can say prayers well enough, calling itself religious for so doing, and thus satisfying conscience. But "the flesh" has no desire or strength for the prayer that strives after an intimate knowledge of God—that rejoices in fellowship with Him, and that continues to lay hold of His strength. So, finally, it comes to this—"the flesh" must be denied and crucified.

The Christian who is still carnal has neither disposition nor strength to follow after God. He rests satisfied with the prayer of habit or custom; but the glory, the blessedness of secret prayer is a hidden thing to him, till some day his eyes are opened, and he begins to see that "the flesh," in its disposition to turn away from God, is the arch-enemy which makes powerful prayer impossible for him. . . .

I had once at a conference spoken on the subject of prayer, and made use of strong expressions about the enmity of "the flesh" as a cause of prayerlessness. After the address, the minister's wife said that she thought I had spoken too strongly. She also had to mourn over too little desire for prayer, but she knew her heart was sincerely set on seeking God. I showed her what the Word of God said about "the flesh," and that everything which prevents the reception of the Spirit is nothing else than a secret work of "the flesh."

Oh, my brethren, do not seek to find in circumstances the explanation of this prayerlessness over which we mourn; seek it where God's Word declares it to be—in the hidden aversion of the heart to a holy God.—Andrew Murray.

In a garden
Was a tree,
Rich with fruit, a token given;
Love's free choice so soon abused;
Still closer fellowship refused:
In a garden.
—C.M.C.
`

27

Bitterness Hinders Prayer

When ye stand praying, forgive, if ye have ought against any (Mark 11:25).

Let none of you imagine evil in your hearts against his neighbour (Zech. 8:17).

You have noticed that Jesus speaks much about prayer and also speaks much about forgiveness. But have you noticed how, over and over again, He couples these two—prayer and forgiveness? I used to wonder why. I do not so much now. Nearly everywhere evidence keeps slipping in of the sore spots. And continually the evidence keeps sifting in, revealing the thin skin, raw flesh, wounds never healed over, and some jaggedly open, almost everywhere one goes. Jesus' continual references reveal how strikingly alike is the oriental and the occidental—the first and the twentieth centuries.—S. D. Gordon.

I heard a knock I knew. I said,
"Lord Jesus, do come in. Come in."
He said, "The door is locked."
It was. . . . I turned the key.
I heard Him touch the handle
    and a crack of light appeared.
"Come in, Lord Jesus. Please come in."
"Something is against the door," He said,
"It will not move!"
I looked. I saw a dark, crude bundle
I had not known was there—an ugly bundle,
    hateful to the touch.
I glanced inside and saw the rancid unforgiveness
    of a wrong.

I pushed it back, flung wide the door, and light
  poured in as
Jesus stepped inside my house and greeted me.
                                        —Jane Emerson.

An insuperable barrier to answered prayer is the spirit of strife and bitterness.

Job had to pray for his very enemies before God could turn his captivity, and had to banish from his heart every particle of bitter feeling towards the men who had tormented him through months of sickness, with their ignorance, misconstruction, and offensive interference. And when he did, God turned his captivity and restored him to more than his former blessings (Job. 42:10).

One reason why the disciples could not claim the casting out of the demon from the suffering child was that they had disputed by the way which should be the greatest. The spirit of cherished animosity, lurking prejudice, sullen vindictiveness, or cold disdain, will as effectually obstruct our intercourse and intimacy with Heaven as a speck upon the crystalline lens of the eye will obstruct our vision, or the crossing of wires of the electric machinery will leave us in darkness.

There are a great many crossed wires in the Church of Christ and the consequence is dark hearts and mournful cries: "Hath God forgotten to be gracious?" (Psalm 77:9). "How long wilt thou be angry against the prayer of thy people?" (Psalm 80:4). Just this long, brother—"If thou bring thy gift to the altar, and there rememberest that thy brother hath ought against thee; leave there thy gift before the altar, and go thy way; first be reconciled to thy brother, and then come and offer thy gift" (Matt. 5:23, 24).—A. B. Simpson.

Beauty of Delayed Answers

If ye then, being evil, know how to give good gifts unto your children, how much more shall your Father which is in heaven give good things to them that ask him? (Matt. 7:11).

My prayer is unto thee, O LORD, in an acceptable time: O God, in the multitude of thy mercy hear me (Psa. 69:13).

Prayers are commonly divided into two classes—those which are conformable to the will of God and those which are not. The Psalmist would suggest a third class belonging to neither the one nor the other. He says there may be prayers which are not conformable to the will of God today, but which will be tomorrow. There is, according to him, an acceptable time for the answering of certain prayers. He does not mean that there is an acceptable time for **praying.** The Heavenly Father appreciates prayer whether He can respond to it or not. The limitation is not to our petitions, but to God's answers.

We often ask things which are in accordance with God's will, but for which we are not ready. A young child asks his father for a knife. Now, that is a possession within the rights of a human being. It is a possession which one day will be of great use to the petitioner for the cutting of knots which cannot be untied. But today it will cut not the string but the finger. I am quite sure that the father will for the present refuse the prayer; he will lay up the desired gift in a safe treasury, awaiting the time when its possession will cease to be a danger. It has been asked at a season which is not acceptable.

Even so, there are special seasons for the gifts of the Heavenly Father. Many a man asks in April a gift of Divine fruit that will only be ripe in June. Take the case of Paul. Immediately after his conversion he prayed for a mission, "Lord, what wouldst Thou have me to do?" He was answered by being sent into the solitudes of Arabia. Was the gratification of his prayer denied, then? No, it was postponed. He had asked at an unacceptable time. He had desired for April the fruits

30

of June. He was not ready for a mission. The light from Heaven had overheated him. He needed to be cooled down ere he could deal with the practical wants of men. Accordingly, God prepared for him a place in the wilderness where he could rest and ponder. The mission was coming, but it was coming with the developed years; it was hid in the bosom of the Father till the acceptable time.

My Father, help me to learn that I am heir to possessions which exceed my present holding! They exceed my present **power** to hold—they are waiting for my summer. Do I ever thank Thee for the blessings which Thou postponest? I am afraid not. I am like the prodigal: I want to get **all at once** the portion that falleth to me; and, where it is not given, I deem it is refused. Teach me, O Lord, the beauty of Thy delayed answers.—George Matheson.

In the moment of its crying
    Came no answer to my heart,
But, long-deferred, it came with blessing
    In a quiet place apart.
Seldom in the midst of toiling
    Do we reap our recompense.
It may come when hands are folded
    In a sunset hour long hence.
Not in thunderous crash of earthquake,
    Not in whirlwind or in fire,
Not in voice of sounding trumpet
    Does God speak our deep desire.
But with strife and fretting over—
    Waiting—all serene and still,
We may hear the whispered message
    Teaching us His perfect will.
When we school our hearts to patience
    God reveals His better way.
Proving oft that His tomorrow
    Is far better than today.
          —Kathryn Blackburn Peck.

Await God's Appointment

It is yet for a time appointed (Dan. 11:35).

For the vision is yet for an appointed time, but at the end it shall speak, and not lie: though it tarry wait for it; because it will surely come, it will not tarry (Hab. 2:3).

Delays are not refusals. Many a prayer is registered, and underneath it the words—"My time is not yet come." God has a set time and way, as well as a set purpose.

The loftiest level of answer is where there is absolutely no sign that God hears or cares. With all the repeated, importunate call, there seems to be none that regards the cry, as with the Baal worshippers on Carmel. The Hearer of Prayer keeps silence. Unbelief would say that the Throne of His Glory is disgraced. Years pass by, and life's morning has reached noon, and noon has sunk to night, and there has been no sensible relief. When faith survives such a trial, and still triumphs in God, it rises to the highest level of the sublime, resting calmly on the changeless Word and character of God. It asks no sign, no voice, no vision, willing to wait for explanation, till the eternal morning dawns and all the shadows flee away!

I asked Mr. Müller, a little before his death, whether he had ever prayed for a long time for a blessing, with no answer. He replied with his wonted precision, that, for more than sixty-five years and four months, he had besought God for the conversion of two men, yet in their sins. But he added: "I shall meet them both in Heaven. My Heavenly Father would not lay on me the burden of two souls for so many years, had He no purposes of mercy concerning them!" He died without the sight, but without the doubt, a rare example of a faith that could repose upon the immutable Promiser, though more than three score years of apparently vain supplication had put both faith and patience to the test.—A. T. Pierson.

When Samuel Pollard had spent just one year in his new role as missionary in China, something unusual was promised to him. He was only twenty-four years of age and was about to engage in a ten-day special Mission. A week of prayer preceded these efforts. Tuesday, the ninth day, was spent in fasting and the entire night was spent in prayer. He writes to a friend: "I shall never forget it. Our room was filled with glory, and I had a manifestation such as I had never realized before. The glory came down and so filled me that I felt the Holy Ghost from my head to the soles of my feet. I had a promise at that meeting that we are going to have thousands of souls. Mind, I believe that from the bottom of my heart. Some folks may say, 'He's a fool!' Let them, we'll have our thousands. 'He's gone mad.' So be it, but we'll have our thousands. 'He's young and enthusiastic.' Yes, glory be to God, I am, and we'll have our thousands."

Did God keep His promise? Yes, but first there was much to be accomplished in Pollard's youthful character. If the promise were fulfilled prematurely, he might worship "fruit" rather than follow on to know the Lord. The testing of faith and the trying of his soul were all necessary before the promised gift was given. Then, it came. After sixteen long years the answer came.

Pollard's biographer tells how four Miao scouts came and told the missionaries of a whole tribe waiting for the new teaching. They swarmed round the missionary for tuition, advice, and counsel. Samuel's wife, fearing for his health, advised him to go up and lock the bedroom door, but what was her surprise to find later that twelve tribesmen were seated round his bed with their books, so happy to be privileged to have their teacher all to themselves. God had kept His promise, but it was for a time appointed.

For the Asking

Ye have not, because ye ask not (James 4:2).

Ask, and it shall be given you (Matt. 7:7).

"Power belongeth unto God," but all that belongs to God we can have for the asking. God holds out His full hands and says: "Ask, and it shall be given you. . . . If ye then, being evil, know how to give good gifts unto your children, how much more shall your Father which is in heaven give good things to them that ask him?" (Matt. 7:7, 11).

The poverty and powerlessness of the average Christian finds its explanation in the words of the apostle James: "Ye have not, because ye ask not" (Jas. 4:2). "Why is it," many a Christian is asking, "that I make such poor progress in my Christian life?" "Neglect of prayer," God answers. "You have not, because you ask not." "Why is it there is so little fruit in my ministry?" asks many a discouraged minister. "Neglect of prayer," God answers again. "You have not, because you ask not." "Why is it," many, both ministers and laymen, are asking, "that there is so little power in my life and service?" And again God answers: "Neglect of prayer. You have not, because you ask not."

God has provided for a life of power and a work of power on the part of every child of His. He has put His own infinite power at our disposal, and has proclaimed over and over again, in a great variety of ways in His Word, "Ask, and ye shall receive."

How little time the average Christian spends in prayer! We are too busy to pray, and so we are too busy to have power. We have a great deal of activity but we accomplish little; many services, but few conversions; much machinery, but few results. The power of God is lacking in our lives and in our work. We have not, because we ask not. Many professed Christians confessedly do not believe in the power

34

of prayer. It is quite the fashion with some to contemptuously contrast the pray-ers with the do-ers—forgetting that in the history of the Church the real do-ers have been pray-ers, that the men who have made the glorious part of the Church's history have been without exception men of prayer.—Torrey.

I have been in that old church in New England where Jonathan Edwards preached his great sermon, "Sinners in the hands of an angry God." He had a little manuscript which he held up so close to his face that they could not see his countenance. But as he went on and on, the people in the crowded church were tremendously moved. One man sprang to his feet, rushed down the aisles, and cried: "Mr. Edwards, have mercy!" Other men caught hold of the backs of the pews lest they should slip into perdition. I have seen the old pillars around which they threw their arms, when they thought the Day of Judgment had dawned upon them. The power of that sermon is still felt in the United States today. But there is a bit of history behind it. For three days Edwards had not eaten a mouthful of food; for three nights he had not closed his eyes in sleep. Over and over again, he had been saying to God: "Give me New England! Give me New England!" And when he rose from his knees, and made his way into the pulpit they say that he looked as if he had been gazing straight into the face of God. They say that before he opened his lips to speak, conviction fell upon his audience.—J. Wilbur Chapman.

To aim aright at the liberty of the children of God requires a continual acting of faith—of a naked faith in a naked promise or declaration. By a naked faith in a naked promise I do not mean a bare assent that God is faithful, and that such a promise in the Book of God may be fulfilled in me, but rather a bold, hearty, steady, venturing of my soul, body, and spirit upon the truth of the promise with an appropriating ACT!—John Fletcher.

Hold God's Character True

It was impossible for God to lie (Heb. 6:18).

Yea, let God be true, but every man a liar (Rom. 3: 4).

But without faith it is impossible to please him: for he that cometh to God must believe that he is, and that he is a rewarder of them that diligently seek him (Heb. 11:6).

Human sin began with loss of faith in God. When our mother Eve listened to Satan's sly innuendoes against the character of God she began to entertain a doubt of His integrity, and right there the doors were opened to the incoming of every possible evil, and darkness settled upon the world.

The Bible talks about man's being alienated from and an enemy to God. Should this sound harsh or extreme you have only to imagine your closest personal friend coming to you and stating in cold seriousness that he no longer has any confidence in you. "I do not trust you. I have lost confidence in your character. I am forced to suspect every move you make." Such a declaration would instantly alienate friends by destroying the foundation upon which every friendship is built. Until your former friend's opinion of you had been reversed there could be no further communion. Only a restored faith could bring about a restored friendship.

Now, it is well known that people do not go boldly to God and profess that they have no confidence in Him, and no one except the rare professional unbeliever is willing to witness publicly to his low view of God. The frightful thing, however, is that people everywhere act out their unbelief with a consistency that is more convincing than words.

Idolatry is the supreme sin and unbelief is the child of idolatry. Both are libels on the character of the Most High and the Most Holy. "He that believeth not God hath made him a liar," wrote the apostle

John. A God who lies is a God without character, and where there is no character there can be no confidence.

The joyous message of Christianity is that there is a way back from this place of unbelief and alienation. "He that cometh to God must believe that he is, and that he is a rewarder of them that diligently seek him." The Gospel message declares that the wronged God took the wrong upon Himself in order that the one who committed the wrong might be saved.

Repentance is, among other things, a sincere apology to God for distrusting Him so long, and faith is throwing oneself upon Christ in complete confidence. Thus by faith reconciliation is achieved between God and man.*—A. W. Tozer.

Our limitless trust in God seems to satisfy Him as nothing else can do, because it corresponds with His eternal faithfulness, it honors His veracity, and is a constant silent worship of all His perfections.

God forever honors those who believe Him. He has organized us on a pattern of trust, and not to trust ourselves in God is to derange the very plan of our creation. Faith in God is at once the sweetest necessity, the sublimest duty, and the greatest privilege of a creature toward his Creator.—G. D. Watson.

The first requirement of prayer is to **believe**.

Believe that God is and that "he is a rewarder of them that diligently seek him."

Believe that God is alive and therefore has power—not only for Peter's deliverance, but for ours.

Believe that God is love and that He cares for His own.

Believe that God is power and therefore no power can stand against Him.

Believe that God is truth and therefore cannot lie.

Believe that God is king and that He will never abdicate His throne or fail in His promise.—Leonard Ravenhill.

*Excerpted from *The Alliance Witness*. Used by permission.

The Unwavering Law of Faith

Jesus saith unto her, Said I not unto thee, that, if thou wouldest believe, thou shouldest see the glory of God? (John 11:40).

Cast not away therefore your confidence, which hath great recompense of reward. For ye have need of patience, that, after ye have done the will of God, ye might receive the promise (Heb. 10:35, 36).

Through all God's dealings with men there is one unwavering law: "by faith," "by faith," "by faith." "Said I not unto thee, that, if thou wouldest believe, thou shouldest see," is the Savior's gentle reproach to those who would work and walk by sight. And God's order and ordination in this life of faith must ever be, "believe that you may see; believe that you may have." "Let us kneel our way through life," said the old saint, "for our knees are Heaven's knockers." This is but another way of putting the same fact that "asking" of God is so much more potent than "doing" by man, because it results in "doing" by God.—Northcote Deck.

"Believing, ye shall receive." The faith-heroes of old "through faith . . . obtained promises," and there is no new way of obtaining them. Is it any wonder that, when we stagger at any promise of God through unbelief, we do not receive it? Not that faith merits the answer, or in any way earns it or works it out, but God has made believing a condition of receiving, and the Giver has a sovereign right to choose His own terms of gift.—Frances Ridley Havergal.

Now learn to hold on by faith for just what you need, and the deeper the need the faster hold on! Oh, if I had only done so more persistently through life, instead of letting the sense of my own weakness dishearten my faith, what a different experience mine would have been. Ah, there is no teaching like experience! You try and learn wisdom by mine. Be a bold believer, and the more you feel your own need, the closer cling to Him as your all and in all, able to magnify His grace where sin hath abounded, and His strength where there is no might.

Remember it is the blood that cleanses the soul. Works meet for repentance is one thing; the faith that heals is another; both are indispensable. The little child or the vilest sinner who dares trust for a full salvation, gets it, while the most careful, principled, and determined disciple who doubts, misses it. God cannot help it; He is bound to give or withhold according to our faith. It is not arbitrary on His part. In the very nature of the case, it is the only line on which He can meet us. I believe if He could have saved us in an easier way, He would have done so, but there was no other way.—Catherine Booth.

Entering a new year, David Livingstone wrote in his diary the prayer that it might be "a year of great believing." This ought to be the overmastering desire of every one of us as we cross the threshold of another year.—Selected.

> Faith is the grasping of Almighty power;
> The hand of man laid on the arm of God;
> The grand and blessed hour
> In which the things impossible to me
> Become the possible, O Lord, through Thee.
> —Anna E. Hamilton.

The great things which the Bible says of faith, it says of it only because it is the channel, the medium, the condition, by and on which the real power, which is Jesus Christ Himself, acts upon us.

It is not the window, but the sunshine that floods this building with light. It is not the opened hand, but the gift laid in it that enriches the pauper. It is not the poor leaden pipe but the water that flows through it that fills the cistern. . . . It is not your faith, but the Christ Whom your faith brings into your heart and conscience, that purges the one and makes the other void of offence toward God and man.
—Alexander Maclaren.

Authority
to Take

Behold, I give unto you power . . . over all the power of the enemy: and nothing shall by any means hurt you (Luke 10:19).

We should use this authority given to us; use it in Jesus' great Name! Use it as the Holy Spirit guides; use it as the need comes in our lives, and in the opposition that is aroused by service. We have authority to take from the enemy everything he is holding back. The chief way of taking is by prayer, and by whatever action prayer leads us to. The cry that should be ringing out today is this great cry of "Take, in Jesus' great Name."

In my Master's Name, I would speak out this message of His, all anew to every follower of His in any need or stress: to those out on the far-flung thin, red firing line of the foreign mission field, in the midst of Africa, of China, of India; to those in the midst of London's slums and streets, in the thick and drive of New York's push and scramble; to anyone and everyone, wherever the stress of sin and of need is being felt.

This is His message to you today. Listen keenly: "I, Jesus, have given you authority over all the power of the enemy. I have the authority. I have won it for you. I give it to you. Use it in My name! Greater works shall ye do because I am with the Father in the place of authority, and you shall act in My place, even as I acted in your place."

Asking means taking! It doesn't mean pleading with God as though to persuade Him. He is more eager than we. It means claiming as our very own whatever is needed. It means taking possession by faith of what our great Captain has won back for us.

The last message of our Lord's lips, on Olivet, fits in here with peculiar power: "All authority hath been given unto me in heaven and

40

on earth. Go ye therefore." That little preposition "on" in "on the earth" could accurately be made to read "over." He has been given all authority on the earth and over the earth. It is because of that authority that we are bidden to "go." We go because of His authority. We go, authorized as His plenipotentiaries. That "go" underlies all Christian service. As we "go" we will need not only power but authority, for every step of our ongoing is contested. In that authority we are to go, and to take what is our rightful possession, in the Name of our Substitute-Victor.

As your service leads you on to a bit of ground that is held by the forces of evil, remember this: that bit of ground belongs to man, to be held by him for God. It has been lost through disobedience. But it has been won back by Jesus, the Victor. You have the right to step in and say, "I take, in the name of the Lord Jesus, I take this back for Him: I take the life of this man, for whom my Master gave His blood."

But—the taking must be as deep as your life; it must be as intense as the opposition. Satan is a stiff fighter: he doesn't yield, except what he must. The taking must be definite. Prayer must always be definite. The devil does not yield until he must. He is a stubborn fighter. Prayer must be persistent. The taking must be as insistent as the enemy is persistent, and just a bit more, and that is where the fight comes.—A. J. Gordon.

And he did not many mighty works there because of their unbelief (Matt. 13:58).

"Pray Out" Lies; "Pray In" Truth

This day is a day of trouble, and of rebuke, and of blasphemy: for the children are come to the birth, and there is not strength to bring forth. . . . Lift up thy prayer (Isa. 37:3, 4).

Thou hast prayed to me against Sennacherib; . . . This is the word which the LORD hath spoken concerning him; . . . I will defend this city (Isa. 37:21, 22, 35).

Prayer is not merely a closet exercise of personal communion, but an acting with God in His battle against evil. Are we taking up the challenge of Satan in our own home, with its tests and trials? In our Church, with its measure of indifference and spiritual deadness? In the land, with its manifestly increasing demon possession? In the world, with its frequent exhibitions of satanic power and fury? Or are we letting things drift? Are we passively submitting to the oppression and antagonism of the powers of darkness, throwing up our hands in a confession of impotence and ignorance of how to act; or are we alert, as Paul and Epaphras were, "labouring fervently in prayer," and setting ourselves aggressively in union with the Holy Spirit, to resist the foe? . . .

When we slacken, the powers of darkness press in. When we fail to pray, the power-house of the Church shuts its door. Nothing is more needed today than companies of Christian people everywhere, who can pray, and persist in prayer. The philosophy of prayer, rightly understood, will impress upon our minds the infinite value to God of a spirit which has learned, in light or darkness, to "continue steadfastly in prayer."

Our responsibility, because of our privilege, is to hold in alliance with the Holy Spirit, the fact and power of the "finished work of Christ," without cessation, over him and his hosts, his methods and his works, until victory has been gained. It puts force into prayer to claim, on the ground of the Blood shed, the loosening of the devil's grip, the beating back of the "rulers of darkness," and the success of righteousness and truth.

Do not pray only for the blessing of God in Christian work, but with equal might and faith pray against the blight of the kingdom of evil. Pray out lies: pray in truth. Pray out the forces of deception and destruction: pray in the life and light of the Lord.

Prayer can not only bring in revival, but it can push out Satan from any ground he has gained in a life or a church or a work, by wielding through implicit, bold, triumphant faith the victory of the Cross against him and every expression of his evil power. Standing in the gap, according to the need of God, it must constantly be borne in mind that passivity of spirit and will is fatal. The activity of all God-given powers is requisite, if the Holy Spirit is to find the human channels through which He can bring to a glorious consummation the longings of the divine heart.—Gordon B. Watt.

Armor thou hast, oh! haste to use,
Ere thou the skill to use it lose;
Powerless thou art if thou refuse
    To arm thee with this panoply.
Though called to wrestle here below
Against a mighty three-fold foe,
Perpetual conquests thou shall know,
    Equipp'd, thou art invincible.
Great, great shall thy rejoicing be,
Ceaseless thy boast of victory,
Till thou thy King in glory see,
    Through Whom thou art omnipotent.
        —Phoebe Palmer.

If thy people go out to battle against their enemy, whithersoever thou shalt send them, and shall pray unto the LORD . . . then hear thou in heaven their prayer and their supplication, and maintain their cause (1 Kings 8:44, 45).

Alert, Prayer Battalions!

For the weapons of our warfare are not carnal, but mighty through God to the pulling down of strong holds (2 Cor. 10:4).

Thou comest to me with a sword, and with a spear, and with a shield: but I come to thee in the name of the LORD of hosts (1 Sam. 17:45).

Prayer is the final armament. Prayer is the all-inclusive strategy of war. Prayer is the ultimate weapon of God's people. Prayer is to be persevered in. Prayer is to be watchfully engaged in day and night. The prayer battalions are to be ever on the alert. They are to be ever active. God's army is to pray always with every form of spiritual prayer. They are to use the sword of the Spirit and to pray in the Spirit.

Prayer in the Spirit will obtain the strategy of the Spirit, His divine guidance for our spiritual warfare. Prayer in the Spirit is to arm every warrior for God. Every Christian is to share in the prayer battle. The Spirit may guide in various spiritual forms of battle but prayer is the constant, all-inclusive, all-conquering, form of battle. "Praying always with all prayer and supplication" is the message of God (Eph. 6:18).

Prayer is a form of spiritual bombing to saturate any area before God's army of witnesses begin their advance. Prayer is the barrage to drive back the demon hosts which are determined to stop the triumph of Christ. Prayer is the invincible force to break down every opposing wall, to open every iron gate and every fast-closed door. Prayer penetrates every curtain of darkness. Prayer crumbles every bastion of darkness. Prayer demolishes every fortress of hell. Prayer is the all-conquering, invincible weapon of the army of God. Therefore Jesus, our victorious Captain, lives to intercede.—Dr. Wesley Duewel.

Stand back!

The workman moves a lever, and
The wrecker's swinging ball
Thuds on old halls.
Debris cascades
In bludgeoned heaps,
The wall is down.

Stand back!

With prayer
The workman puts his hands
On levers that direct
Power tools
For other shatterings.
Other walls go down.

Stand back and kneel!
—Elva McAllaster.

Satan's weapons have been hung up in derision on the cross of Calvary and Satan himself put on exhibition there like the brazen serpent of old, as a mere empty, fangless thing, as powerless to harm as that metal figure hung up in the wilderness of Sinai. Beloved, are you thus treating your spiritual enemy in the light of the cross of Calvary, or are you letting the mighty victory of the Captain of your salvation go for naught? . . .

God wants men and women today on whom He can depend, to stand as bulwarks and battlements against the shocks of hell's artillery—men and women of whom He can say, "Upon this rock have I built my church, and the gates of hell shall not prevail against it." Shall we, beloved, be not only conquerors, but trusted soldiers whom God can use as His battle-axes and His weapons of war, as His mighty iron-clads, to carry the battle to the very ships of the enemy, not fearing their hardest blows and hurling against them the thunderbolts of His victorious power?—A. B. Simpson.

Vanguard of
an Invasion Force

Pray ye . . . . Thy kingdom come. Thy will be done (Matt. 6:9, 10).

The kingdom of heaven suffereth violence, and the violent take it by force (Matt. 11:12).

The kingdoms of this world are become the kingdoms of our Lord (Rev. 11:15).

Don Richardson in a Memorial Service for the martyred missionaries in West Irian had this inspired explanation to give for the hatred and abuse heaped upon the loving ministries of the Christian. This holds true in other than heathen lands but merely is shown in a more polished manner:

"We may well ask, 'Why is it that people who are loyal to Jesus Christ, who endeavor to be as He was, holy, harmless, undefiled—people whose desire is to live and teach the ethic of Heaven itself—why should they be, in every age, the objects of such furious hatred?'

"There are, perhaps, many reasons. I will name what I believe is the main one. The ungodly of this world persecute the body of Christ because they instinctively recognize that body as the vanguard of an invasion from another world, a world diametrically opposed to this one. The ungodly are fighting to hold this planet against this invasion, even though it is an invasion by the greatest love and goodness that ever was. The ungodly want to keep this planet a place where they can practice independent meaning in rebellion against God, even though the penalty for that rebellion is death itself, and so they resent every encroachment from that other world where the rule is that men practice dependent meaning in submission to God.

"Some imaginative men have speculated about the possibility that this world may some day be invaded from outside itself. Little do they realize that an invasion of this world occurred two thousand years ago, an invasion far more subtle, far more sophisticated, far more certain of success than anything that the wildest flight of man's imagination could conceive. The **Incarnation** of Jesus Christ was that invasion and He is still carrying on His conquest, not by bringing in armies to suppress the earth, but by transforming His enemies into citizens of His kingdom through His Gospel."—Helen Manning.

The continuance of this invasion is largely maintained by the secret prayer warriors described by S. D. Gordon:

"The victor's best ally in this conflict is the man, who while he remains down on the battlefield, puts his life in full touch with his Savior-Victor, and then incessantly, insistently, believingly claims victory in Jesus' name. He is the one foe among men whom Satan cannot withstand. He is projecting an irresistible spirit force into the spirit realm. Satan is obliged to yield. We are so accustomed through history's long record to seeing victories won through force, physical force, alone, that it is difficult for us to realize that moral force defeats as the other never can. . . .

"Every time such a man prays it is a waving of the red-dyed flag of Jesus Christ above Satan's head in the spirit world. Every such man who freely gives himself over to God and gives himself up to prayer is giving God a new spot in the contested territory on which to erect His banner of victory."

Christian to arms! Behold in sight
The treacherous, threatening sons of might;
To arms! or thou art put to flight;
   Attest thy glorious chivalry.
Each moment's respite sees thy wrong,
Supinely thou hast dwelt too long.
Thy foes, alas! they grow more strong.
   Arise! Acquit thee valiantly!
              —Selected.

Costliness of Evicting Satan

Thy seed shall possess the gate of his enemies (Gen. 22:17).

How can one enter into a strong man's house, and spoil his goods, except he first bind the strong man? and then he will spoil his house (Matt. 12:29).

If as God's servants we are only laboring for others we are missing God's first aim in creation, which was to supply not merely man's need but His own. For as we have said already, the creation of man was to meet the need of God. Thus if today we are going to meet God's need we must go a step further and deal with Satan himself. We must steal back from him his power, evict him from his territory, spoil him of his goods, and set free his captives—for God. The question is not merely, "Of what account are we in the winning of souls?" Rather is it, "Of what account are we in the realm of principalities and powers?" And for that there is a price to pay.

It is often possible to move men when it is quite impossible to move Satan. The plain fact is that it costs much more to deal with Satan than to win souls. It demands an utterness of spirit Godward that in itself effectually deprives Satan of any moral ground in us he may claim to possess. This is the costly thing. God in His merciful love for the lost can often bypass and overlook in His servants what one might justly feel to be appalling weakness and even failure. But while He may do this for the soul-winner, when it comes to our dealing with the devil it is another matter.

Evil spirits can see right through the witness of man. They can tell when it is compromised by being half-hearted or insincere. They are aware when we are holding back a part of the price. Looking at us they are under no illusions as to whom they can safely defy or ignore; and conversely, they know perfectly well against whom they are powerless. "Jesus I know, and Paul I know; but who are ye?"

(Acts19:15). Because they believe, they know when to tremble. And let me say this: since our most important task is their overthrow, it is better always that we should have the witness of evil powers than the praise of men.

But the price of this witness to the principalities and powers is, I repeat, an utterness of allegiance to God that is unqualified. To entertain our own opinions or desires, to prefer our own variant and contrary choices, is simply to present the enemy with his advantage. It is, in short, to throw the game away. In any other sphere there may perhaps—I do not know—be room among our motives for something of self-interest, without appreciable loss. But never, and I repeat never, in this. Without such utterness for God nothing can be achieved, for without it we make even God powerless against His enemy.

So I say it once again: the demand is very high. Are you and I here on earth, utterly committed, utterly given to God Himself? And because this is so, are we tasting even now the powers of that future glorious age? Are we reclaiming territory from the prince of this world for the One Whose alone it rightly is?—Watchman Nee.

I found that my own carnality and selfishness had given the ground they held to these monsters of hell. I myself had invited them in. I must get rid of "self" else there could be no hope of final victory. These powers of darkness (demons are as real to me now as God Himself) which were oppressing me to the point of despair, were standing on the very ground which secret selfishness had conceded to them.

How was I to get rid of this "self-life" which had so long been standing out against Christ and making a way for the enemy to come in like a flood? Ah, had I but known of that "Standard," the Cross, which must be lifted up against this prince of darkness!

Such a struggle as mine would never issue in victory except the Cross be given the place of absolute supremacy in my life and ministry.—F. J. Huegel.

A Spiritual Man
for Spirit-Wrestling

We wrestle not against flesh and blood, but
against principalities,
against powers,
against the rulers of the darkness of this world,
against spiritual wickedness (wicked spirits) in high places (Eph.
6:12).

Who can fight this prayer battle? A very short answer can be given to that question. The New Testament makes clear that the wrestler with the forces of evil must be a spiritual man, for only he can understand the battle and the equipment necessary for it. A carnal Christian begins the fight defeated. A natural man cannot side with God. But what is a spiritual man?

The late Dr. J. Elder Cumming described him as "a man in whom not only his own spirit takes the lead in self-government and discipline, but in whom the Spirit of God is dwelling in person and power; and he does this above all—he has been and is 'receiving' the Spirit of God as in control and mastership, redressing the balance of powers within, and through the man's own spirit subordinating all the carnal and worldly, bringing him into conformity with Christ."

His own spirit, gathering to its aid all human faculties, under the government and enlightenment of the Holy Spirit, moves out on to the spiritual battlefield to stand with God, and through prayer, make possible the interposition of divine powers to crown with success the work of grace.

But where is this prayer battle to be won? In the closet, in the quietness of personal communion with God. To be in touch with Him is to come into the light, and to be there is to see what He sees. . . . The battle against the powers of darkness must be won on the believer's knees. "Brother," wrote Dr. Hudson Taylor to Dr. Goforth, "if you are to win that province (North Honan), you must go forward on your knees." The closet must give to prayer vitality, and vitality springs from Calvary in action in the believer's life. The fight against the foes of God must be joined to unflinching opposition to all known sin. No minimizing or toleration of personal inherent weakness can be permitted, save at great peril.

If the Cross is not a sanctifying force in the heart, it will give no driving, delivering momentum in the prayer battle in the world. In the measure in which personal identification with Christ in resistance to sin and self is real and deep, will there be victory over the schemes and agencies of Satan. The power of prayer, to effect a spiritual revolution in a church or nation, depends upon the length we are prepared to go in allowing the Holy Spirit to apply to our own characters the revealing, as well as the sanctifying force of the Cross. . . .

Full surrender to God for the work of intercession is without doubt the first and clamant imperative. The basis of victorious prayer, as it is equally the ground of triumphant living, is disclosed in the command, "Yield yourselves unto God." Calvary is meaningless or resultless, unless it creates such a spirit of yieldedness as permits of the Holy Spirit accomplishing the purpose of the sacrifice of the Savior.

Prayer is translated into a real fighting force against evil, as the Cross, through the Spirit of God, succeeds in making actual in the life of the believer freedom from the domination of the self-life. In the measure in which Satan can find the old Adam nature his ally in the heart, must there be a hindrance to the power of God, and a resultant weakness in the attitude and action of the believer. Personal victory over every form of sin conditions our ability to stand with God in definite aggressiveness of spirit against His enemy.—Gordon B. Watt.

Praying
Kingdom Builders

These all continued with one accord in prayer and supplication, with the women (Acts 1:14).

And they continued stedfastly in the apostles' doctrine . . . and in prayers (Acts 2:42).

We need time for prayer, unhurried time, daily time, time enough to forget about how much time it is. I do not mean now—rising in the morning at the very last moment, and dressing, it may be hurriedly, and then kneeling a few moments so as to feel easier in mind—not that. I do not mean last thing at night when you are jaded and fagged and almost between the sheets, and then remember and look up a verse and kneel a few moments—not that. That is good so far as it goes. I am not criticizing that. Better sweeten and sandwich the day with all of that sort you can get in. But just now I mean this: taking time when the mind is fresh and keen, and the spirit sensitive, to thoughtfully pray. We haven't time. Life is so crowded. It must be taken from something else, something important, but still less important than this.

Sacrifice is the continual law of life. The important thing must be sacrificed to the more important. One needs to cultivate a mature judgment, or his strength will be frizzled away in the less important details, and the greater thing go undone, or be done poorly with the fag-ends of strength. If we would become skilled intercessors, and know how to pray simply enough, we must take quiet time daily to get off alone.—S. D. Gordon.

Apostolic men knew well the worth of prayer and were jealous of the most sacred offices which infringed on their time and strength and hindered them from "giving themselves continually to prayer, and to the ministry of the Word." They put prayer first. The Word depends on prayer that it "may have free course, and be glorified." Praying apostles make preaching apostles. God's Gospel has always waited more on prayer than on anything else for its successes. A praying Church is strong though poor in all besides. A prayerless Church is weak though rich in all besides. Praying hearts only will build God's Kingdom. Praying hands only will place the crown on the Savior's head. . . .

Adoniram Judson impressed an empire for Christ and laid the foundations of God's kingdom with imperishable granite in the heart of Burma. He was successful, one of the few men who mightily impressed the world for Christ. Many men of greater gifts and genius and learning than he have made no such impression; their religious work is like footsteps in the sands, but he has engraven his work on the adamant. The secret of its profundity and endurance is found in the fact that he gave time to prayer.

He kept the iron red-hot with prayer, and God's skill fashioned it with enduring power. No man can do a great and enduring work for God who is not a man of prayer, and no man can be a man of prayer who does not give much time to praying.—E. M. Bounds.

> O instruct us how to pray!
> Pour out the supplicating grace,
> And stir us up to seek Thy face.
> We cannot think a gracious thought,
> We cannot feel a good desire,
> Till Thou, Who calledst a world from nought,
> The power into our hearts inspire.
> The promised Intercessor give,
> And let us now Thyself receive.
> —Charles Wesley.

The Key
to Divine Energy

Seek the LORD and his strength, seek his face continually (I Chron. 16:11).

But the people that do know their God shall be strong, and do exploits (Dan. 11:32).

Walker of Tinnevelly, after years of missionary endeavor, resigned from some of his official responsibilities in order to give more time to prayer and evangelistic effort. The local newspaper announced that Rev. T. Walker used to be a hard worker but had now retired to the district to pray. Majoring in the spiritual he was bound to be misunderstood. He wrote a pamphlet on prayer hoping to stir others to the power of prayer. We quote a portion:

"Better, far better, do less work, if need be, that we may pray more, because work done by the rushing torrent of human energy will not save a single soul, whereas work done in vital and unbroken contact with the living God will tell for all eternity.

"The cry is heard from every quarter: 'Over-work. Too much to do.' No charge of idleness can be truly laid against us, as a whole. But how is it that so much of our busy energy appears to be expended all in vain? Holy Scripture, personal experience, the voice of conscience, all these alike suggest at least one answer—we have neglected largely the means which God Himself has ordained for true anointing from on High.

"We have not given prayer its proper place in the plan of our campaign. Has not much time been spent in the school, the office, the village, or the zenana, and little, very little, in the secret chamber? Fellow-missionaries, we have toiled much, but we have prayed little. The energy of the flesh of our intellect, of our position, of our very enthusiasm, this has been allowed to usurp, to a lamentable extent, the place of the one power which can rouse immortal souls from the slumber of eternal death—the might of the living God, the energy of the Holy Ghost.

"How many a day passes by in hundreds of missionary bungalows in one ceaseless, busy stream of work, without any time for quiet intercourse with God, except the few brief minutes snatched in the early morning before the rush begins or the short space allowed in the late evening by exhausted nature!

"How many of us plead for India as Robert Murray McCheyne pleaded for his Dundee congregation, never ceasing to pray for them, even when sickness drove him from them for a time, and turning the very shores of the Sea of Galilee into an oratory, till God opened the windows of Heaven and poured down upon them showers of blessing? Or again, how many of us pray for the souls around us in this heathen land as Robert Aitken prayed for those congregations in which he carried on his mission work, spending hours upon his knees, after a day of busy preaching, beseeching God, with strong crying and tears, to save the souls of men? We all know the importance of prayer and can preach discourses on its efficacy, but do we practice what we preach ourselves?"

"The great battles," says Samuel L. Brengle, "the battles that decide our destiny and the destiny of generations yet unborn, are not fought on public platforms, but in the lonely hours of the night and in moments of agony."

Lord, Keep Me on My Knees

Daniel . . . kneeled upon his knees three times a day (Dan. 6:10).

For this cause I bow my knees unto the Father of our Lord Jesus Christ (Eph. 3:14).

Mary Warburton Booth went out to India full of bright hopes, but after five years of barrenness, she came home on furlough, dispirited and contemplating no return. At a Keswick Convention she was inwardly challenged to return to her field, but with this difference: she would put prayer foremost in the future. Her poem reveals her secret which we would do well to learn and implement in our own sphere of service:

> "God called me out to work for Him,
>   And oh, what joy and love
> Came to my life as I went forth
>   To win for Heaven above.
> As time went on I saw the need,
>   Gross darkness everywhere,
> So in the forefront of my work
>   I supplemented prayer.
> God kept me on to work for Him,
>   And day by day I learned
> How sacred was my blessed task
>   As o'er the lost I yearned.
> With will and purpose on I toiled,
>   Oft questioning—what availed
> This weary striving day by day?
>   In winning souls—I failed.

He kept me on, and on I went,
    And then there came a day
When all was changed—I put it down
    That you might know the way—
He stopped me in my self-planned toil,
    And laid my purpose bare,
And I, ashamed, rebuked, went down
    In agonizing prayer.
He heard me as I turned to Him,
    And He just turned to me,
Took both my hands in His, and said,
    'Great victories you shall see.
The secret is for you to know
    That what you do and where,
The fundamental work for you
    Is prayer, deep prayer, real prayer.'
And oh, the victories He has wrought
    And oh, the souls He won,
When I have prayed right through to God
    He brought them one by one.
Until I look and am amazed,
    For prayer has brought release,
And now I pray, whatever else,
    'Lord, keep me on my knees.'
                    —M. W. Booth.

God sets more value on prayer and communion than labor. The heavenly bridegroom is wooing a wife, not hiring a servant. Prayer brings God out of His secret place to work wonders in the earth . . . to pour Himself through the believer into a world of lost souls.

                    —A. W. Roffe.

The Results of Great Waiting

Our soul waiteth for the LORD: he is our help and our shield (Psa. 33:20).

And thou shalt know that I am the LORD: for they shall not be ashamed that wait for me (Isa. 49:23).

Those that wait upon the LORD, they shall inherit the earth (Psa. 37:9).

Spiritual work is taxing work, and men are loath to do it. Praying, true praying, costs an outlay of serious attention and of time, which flesh and blood do not relish. Few persons are made of such strong fiber that they will make a costly outlay when surface work will pass as well in the market. We can habituate ourselves to our beggarly praying until it looks well to us, at least it keeps up a decent form and quiets conscience—the deadliest of opiates! We can curtail our praying, and not realize the peril till the foundations are gone. Hurried devotions make weak faith, feeble convictions, and questionable piety. To be little with God is to be little for God. To cut short the praying makes the whole religious character short, scrimp, niggardly, and slovenly.

It takes good time for the full flow of God into the spirit. Short devotions cut the pipe of God's full flow. It takes time in the secret places to get the full revelation of God. Little time and hurry mar the picture.

Henry Martyn laments that "want of private devotional reading and shortness of prayer through incessant sermon-making had produced much strangeness between God and his soul." He judged that he had dedicated too much time to public ministrations and too little to private communion with God. He was much impressed with the need of setting apart times for fasting and to devote times for solemn prayer. Resulting from this he records: "Was assisted this morning to pray for two hours.". . .

Our ability to stay with God in our closet measures our ability to stay with God out of the closet. . . . Tarrying in the closet instructs and wins. We are taught by it, and the greatest victories are often the results of great waiting—waiting till words and plans are exhausted, and silent and patient waiting gains the crown. Jesus Christ asks with an affronted emphasis, "Shall not God avenge His own elect which cry day and night unto Him?"—E. M. Bounds.

It is the overloaded hearts that are apt to pray the least.
—William Watson.

"What has been the secret of your marvelous success in India?" was asked not long ago of a fair, delicate, young lady missionary, who had been most marvelously owned of God in work among Telegus. Her answer is worthy of remembrance of all who are toiling for the advancement of the kingdom of Christ at home, as well as abroad. Modestly, but in a way that thrilled all who heard her, she replied:

"I never let my missionary duties, heavy and many though they are, rob me of the time devoted to private devotions and communion with Christ through prayer and His Word. I found it better to limit my time for meals and sleep, rather than the time consecrated to personal communion with God alone. If a sick Hindu came to see me when at prayer, I finished my devotions as usual and ever felt that I was so much the better prepared to prescribe more wisely for the disease; and in this I have never been mistaken."

These are words worthy of being pondered over by us all. In these active days there is so much fuss and flutter, and we seem to be so busy amidst the multitudinous duties that come to us. We cannot, therefore, be too careful in guarding our own soul's interest and the time when we go apart from the world and commune alone with Him Who is the source of our strength.

Barren Busyness

As thy servant was busy here and there, he was gone (1 Kings 20:40).

I must be about my Father's business (Luke 2:49).

The very conditions of a minister's work—which put into his own hands the control of his time and the ordering of his days—impose a peculiar responsibility. If he fritters time away in idleness, if he squanders in desultory reading of the newspaper and magazine reviews those precious morning hours which ought to be rigorously safeguarded for wrestling with the Word of God, if when Sunday comes he offers to his people sermons shoddy with lack of thought, he damages his troth to Christ and dishonors his high calling. He proves himself to be culpably impercipient of the deep spiritual needs and longings of those whom the great Shepherd has committed to his care. He has never heard the inarticulate crying of the hungry flock, "O, refresh us, traveling through this wilderness." He is the hireling who careth not for the sheep.

Beware the professional busy-ness which is but slackness in disguise! The trouble is that we may even succeed in deceiving ourselves. Our diary is crowded. Meetings, discussions, interviews, committees throng the hectic page. We are driven here, there, everywhere by the whirling machinery of good works. We become all things to all men. Laziness? The word, we protest, is not in our vocabulary. Are we not engrossed from morning till night? Do we not conspicuously spend our days under the high pressure of an exacting life? But God, Who searches the heart, knows how much of our outward strenuousness is but a rationalization of a latent slackness. What does it amount to—the whole paraphernalia of good works and religious machinery—if there is lacking the intense concentration on the message which is to deliver men's eyes from tears, their feet from falling, and their souls from death, the lonely wrestling with God at Peniel without which no blessing comes.—James S. Stewart.

Beware of the barrenness of a busy life.—Selected.

"One of Satan's methods today," said the late G. Campbell Morgan, "is starting so many organizations that the Church members have not time for communion with God. The Church is so busy that one cannot move without hearing the clink and the friction of her wheels. Whenever the Church becomes so fussy about her work that she has no time for communion with God, the world looks on, and smiles at her and helps her with her bazaars, and stays from her prayer-meetings. Oh, that God would turn us back to communion with Himself! . . . Oh, that we might make time to sit at His feet!"

"I remember to have read." says J. N. Nisbet, "a book entitled *A Dying Man's Regrets*, and he was a very good and holy man, singularly devoted to the service of his God, and yet what did he say? These are his words: 'Ah! if I were to return to life, I would, with the help of God, and in distrust of myself, give much more time to prayer than I have hitherto done. I would reckon much more upon the effect of that than on my own labor, which, however much it is our duty never to neglect, yet has no strength except so far as it is animated by prayer. I would especially strive to obtain in my prayers that fervor of the Holy Spirit which is not learnt in a day, but is the fruit of a long, and often a painful apprenticeship. Oh, my friends (he added, raising himself with energy on his sick bed) lay hold of the opportunity and redeem it; cultivate new habits of prayer. Bring into prayer, with a spirit of fervor, a spirit also of order and of method that will increase its power, as it increases the power of all human things, and cooperates with Divine agency itself.'"

"Busy"ness Crowds Out Eternal Business

And the care of this world, and the deceitfulness of riches, choke the word, and he becometh unfruitful (Matt. 13:22).

Take heed to yourselves, lest at any time your hearts be overcharged with surfeiting . . . and cares of this life (Luke 21:34).

Oh, how few find time for prayer! There is time for everything else, time to sleep and time to eat, time to read the newspaper and the novel, time to visit friends, time for everything else under the sun, but—no time for prayer, the most important of all things, the one great essential!

Think of Susannah Wesley who, in spite of the fact that she had nineteen children, found time to shut herself in her room for a full hour each day, alone with God. My friends, it is not so much a case of finding time as it is of making time. And we can make time if we will.

—Oswald Smith.

Christ was our great example, leaving the crowd, to talk with His Father. G. H. Lang says: "'But He withdrew Himself in the deserts (plural) and prayed.' This throws His action into strong contrast with the urgency of the thronging crowds: they clamored to be healed and taught, BUT He denied them at that time. The plural 'deserts' shows that the Lord withdrew on several occasions. But Luke stated this yet more distinctly by two participles: 'But He was withdrawing Himself in the deserts and praying.' It was a practice.

"It required urgent grounds thus to neglect opportunities He had Himself created; it required uncommon strength of character to do so. It is not easy to be a thorough imitator of Jesus, a fearless disciple. In mission medical work it has been frequent that a successful operation or cure has brought crowds to the dispensary or hospital. How many doctors have been wise enough or strong enough to retire from the scene for days together to pray—just to pray? It is so easy to reason that now is our opportunity, the tide will not always flow with us thus, we must work while it is day—until vigor is exhausted and even collapse is reached! Indeed, sometimes devoted workers have followed exactly the opposite course to Christ, and have extended their premises and increased their burdens though no extra help was in view.

"'But **He** was withdrawing Himself in the deserts and praying.' He knew that only God has inexhaustible energy."*

Mrs. Howard Taylor tells in her biography how Pastor Hsi, a worker among the opium addicts, felt he must take time out for prayer. "With increasing responsibilities Hsi felt increasingly the need for prayer. From the first he had been prayerful. But now the customary hour, morning and evening, and daily seasons of public worship he found to be insufficient. Longer, more quiet times were needed for waiting upon God, that His mind might be made known and His fullness received. Instead, therefore, of allowing his work to drive him and absorb his time and thoughts, he deliberately set everything aside for hours and sometimes days or nights of prayer—often with fasting. At these times it was that he usually obtained new thoughts and plans for the work, and fresh visions of God's faithfulness, as well as a deeper consciousness of his own insufficiency."

*From the writings of G.H. Lang. By permission.

The Antidote of
Incessant Activity

Wait on the LORD: be of good courage, and he shall strengthen thine heart: wait, I say, on the Lord (Psa. 27:14).

And therefore will the LORD wait, that he may be gracious unto you, and therefore will he be exalted, that he may have mercy upon you: for the LORD is a God of judgment: blessed are all they that wait for him (Isa. 30:18).

Too much business has robbed many a man of deep spirituality and caused him to live on the borderline between righteousness and unrighteousness. It has stolen away the sweetness of Christian love while the conjugal love of home has burned to a smoldering ember.

Too many calls, meetings, conventions, committee meetings, besides the ceaseless round of duties, have stolen from many a minister's soul the sweetness of prayer and have caused the Bible to become dull and uninteresting. The romance of the ministry is gone, and the joy of being a soul-winner is buried in the dust of present activities.

We are in an age in which speed, production, achievement, and creation are the measuring rods by which all men are judged. These, however, are false standards. The eternal God is concerned with **growing a forest of oaks rather than filling the backyard with toadstools.** He is more concerned with character than He is with production, and demands quality despite quantity. Sainthood is produced by long hours in meditating upon God. It takes time spent alone with the Eternal to learn His secrets. Wait upon God; continue to look into His face if you would become like Him. . . .

The great business of Satan is to draw us away from communion with God. Activity absorbs attention, and Self forces Christ from the throne of the soul. It is easier to spend two hours studying figures, blueprints, scientific books, philosophers, than it is to wait quietly upon God in self-abasement.

Ministers who are orthodox, devoted, and busy, need to lay aside many "things" and rekindle the holy glow within their own souls. Do not be so busy running a program that you have no time to wait upon Christ.—Oliver G. Wilson.

> Away with work that hinders prayer,
> 'Twere best to lay it down;
> For prayerless work, however good,
> Will fail to win the crown.
> —Unknown.

Dr. A. T. Pierson called upon a minister who had been hospitalized for six months. Said he to the patient, "My brother, you have been a very busy man. It may be that God has something He has wanted to say to you, but you have been too busy to listen. So God, in goodness and infinite wisdom, had to put you on your back that you might hear His voice and receive His message."

As Dr. Pierson left the hospital, the Lord seemed to say to him, "You, too, have been very active **for** Me and have not taken enough time to be occupied **with** Me!"

Dr. Pierson said, "From that time, I resolved to **practice** what I preached. At the close of each day, I sit for one hour in the quiet of my study, not to speak to the Lord, but to listen to what the Lord has to say to me, and to lay the day's life and work open to the Lord's penetrating gaze and appraisal!"

I will hear what God the LORD will speak: for he will speak peace unto his people, and to his saints: but let them not turn again to folly" (Psa. 85:8).

The Busy Man's Peril

They made me the keeper of the vineyards; but mine own vineyard have I not kept (Song of Solomon 1:6).

In the fulness of his sufficiency he shall be in straits (Job 20:22).

The world is enough to busy us, not to fill us. "In the fulness of his sufficiency he shall be in straits."—T. Watson.

We must make time for meditative habits and communion with God. The soul grows thin in its activities. Says Dean Vaughan, "Many a Christian's incessant action is the grave of his spiritual life."

—Thomas Cook.

"Work is not food for the spirit any more than for the body. Amidst a multitude of works the worker's soul may wither, and his activities will prove this in due time. We must live upon Jesus Christ, not upon energy, upon success, upon notice, upon praise." If we attempt to live upon any of these, we shall have to make the painful confession: "They made me the keeper of the vineyards; but mine own vineyard have I not kept."

Our present object is to point out the dangers attending excessive Christian activity. The first danger is that of spending without replenishing; of multiplying active ministries, and curtailing loving fellowship. We cannot be made a blessing to others without perceiving that virtue is gone out of us, and unless this is constantly renewed by loving communion with Heaven, the service becomes little more than dead work, and the message loses the ring which bespeaks its Divine origin.

There is a fine old mountain in Wales called Plinlimmon. For ages he has been drinking from every cloud that has settled upon his head, until he has become a great reservoir, and from him today there flow five rivers. If we drink from the Invisible and the Eternal, there will flow from us rivers of blessing, fertilizing, gladdening and blessing all around. But if we fail to hold communion with the skies, we shall be guilty of the mockery which holds an empty vessel to the lips of a thirsty man.—J. Gregory Mantle.

Donald Gee, a busy Bible College principal and evangelist, found himself incarcerated for ten weeks in a hospital ward. This enforced quiet produced the most appropriate advice for Christian workers in this over-busy age, which we pass on: "It has become trite to complain that we are living in a day of constant rush. Our trouble is not work, but rush, speed, breathlessness, hurry, and generally hectic living. Everything tempts us to it: we can take a car where we used to walk; we can take a plane where we used to travel by boat; we can phone where we used to write a letter; we read 'Digests' instead of solid books; we can look and listen to others discussing a matter instead of sitting down to a good conversation about it with a few friends of our own.

"Our 'successful' preachers have become those whose diaries have engagements three or four years ahead. The popular evangelist moves from one campaign to another in a tightly packed schedule guarded over by a 'business manager.' It is quite difficult for us smaller fry not to be caught in the net. Yet the result is a multiplicity of nervous complaints among the people at large that take their toll of physical, quite as much as emotional health. Meanwhile the compounders of drugs reap a harvest from the sale of 'tranquilizers' and our mental hospitals have an alarmingly swollen population. . . . I am persuaded that there is a place of spiritual listening for the voice of God. If there is not, then the great Bible phrase 'Waiting on the Lord' becomes almost meaningless. Such 'waiting' involves saying nothing—both quite difficult to people conditioned to ceaseless activity, even in their religious life."

The School
of Silence

I have spoken . . . that in me ye might have peace (John 16:33).

Stand still, and consider the wondrous works of God (Job 37:14).

Be still, and know that I am God. . . . I will be exalted in the earth (Psa. 46:10).

"Be still, and know that I am God." This is part of the Gospel to a busy age. One is struck at once with the contrast betwixt it and the gospel of the world—if so holy a word as "gospel" can rightly be used to describe the world's philosophy. This is what the world says: "Be industrious and know material success." "Be diligent, and know earth's secrets and wisdom." "Be active, and know the joy of living." "Be energetic, and know the delight of mastery." God says, "Be still, and know that I am God." If there is one thing more than another which men, whose hearts are not pure, fear, it is the necessity for quiet thought. Men and women engage in all kinds of activities in order to narcotize their consciences and their memories. They stimulate their jaded senses to fresh endeavors, lest they should be forced to consider their ways before God.—Stuart Holden.

Robert E. Lyons observes that "modern men seem to be afraid of silence. We are conditioned by radio and television on which every minute must be filled with talking or some kind of sound. We are stimulated by the philosophy of keeping on the move all the time—busy, busy, busy. This tends to make us shallow. A person's life can be deepened tremendously by periods of silence, used in the constructive ways of meditation and prayer. Great personalities have spent much time in the silences of life."

Oliver G. Wilson, editor of *Wesleyan Methodist* for many years, relates an interesting experience in his own life: "For some time, things had not been going satisfactorily according to my poor limited vision. World situations were distressing and far beyond any solution that I had to offer. Business was not going as in my judgment it should go. I felt keenly that I had been taken advantage of, and spent much of the night turning restlessly in bed. Tensions, frustrations, impossible situations, disagreement among trusted friends, all plagued me. At the close of the second day, when night had settled and nature was putting itself to bed, there came from memory this portion of the Psalm learned long years ago, 'Be still, and know that I am God.'

"It came with such force, with emphasis upon each word such as no man could give it; my heart melted. A song, seasoned with happy tears, was sung within my soul: 'Be still, and know that I am God.' Very much of our trouble and anxiety arises from our useless chatter, from our ceaseless activity, from our reliance upon our own wisdom. We have a guilty feeling if religion is not doing something. We want progress, but back of progress must be peace. One does not need a brass band to appreciate God. His mercy, His grace, His presence, when realized, overwhelm us."

> Be still sometimes—so still that God may speak,
>   And make His voice heard in thy waiting heart.
> Sometimes the hush of His calm presence seek;
>   From all the world's confusion come apart,
> And silence even praise, and breathe no prayer,
> But only wait for Him to meet thee there.
> Be still sometimes! Be still enough to hear
>   The faintest whisper of His voice, and feel
> The touch of His dear hand, when He draws near,
>   Himself unto thy spirit to reveal.
> God will His deepest truths to thee make known,
> Only when thou art silent and alone.
>   —Edith Hickman Divall.

Prayer—
Mountain Torrents

And the LORD said unto Moses, Come up to me into the mount, and be there: and I will give thee . . . (Exodus 24:12).

And he gave unto Moses, when he had made an end of communing with him upon mount Sinai (Exodus 31:18).

We in the West have had to acknowledge that often God's children in Africa, India, Japan, and China have put us to shame by their complete devotion to God. Sadhu Sundar Singh, an Indian Christian who suffered much for Christ's sake, is just such an example. He writes:

"On the mountains, torrents flow right along, cutting their own courses. But on the plains canals have to be dug out painfully by men so that the water might flow. So among those who live on the heights with God, the Holy Spirit makes His way through of His own accord, whereas those who devote little time to prayer and communion with God have to organize painfully."

Daniel Smith, in his short biography of Bakht Singh, brings to our attention another Indian national who was a devoted servant of Jesus. He writes about this man's life on the Mount alone with God, and relates how torrents of spiritual energy flowed from his life, watering the plain below: "I have never seen equaled in any man a life of prayer, and I have moved around the world a good deal. Bakht Singh rises early, sometimes at four a.m., even though he is seldom in bed before midnight. His day begins with several hours of prayer and devotional reading of his Bible. No calls for breakfast must break into his devotional waiting upon the Lord. Throughout the day every matter is brought before the Lord in prayer. No move is made and no journey undertaken without prayer. He never ventures outside without prayer, never enters or leaves a home without prayer, never receives or sends a visitor away without prayer. Nor does this fervent and zealous spirit of prayer ever seem to be thrown off at any time or in any day. His is a true life of prayer. Twenty times a day you may hear the word, 'Shall we pray,' and this prayer is always on the knees.

"His desires in prayer are very vigorous, flowing like a strong stream that cannot stay to creep into little holes or spend their energies in small crevices. Nothing is wasted by flowery language or trifles of no moment. His prayers, though much longer than his letters, are like the sentences of his letters in that they are to the point, falling and rising with swift motion and hungry appetite. No wonder he accomplishes so much. All lies, I am sure, in the terrific, vigorous resolution of this truly wonderful prayer-life. Year in and year out the force of it never seems to be retarded. All who know him will bear testimony of the life and nature and quality of his prayer. Never does he grow weary in prayer. Oh, what a man of prayer! Oh, what prayers!"

Alone upon the mount of God I stand,
        With silenced heart His voice to hear;
'Tis love itself hath led this hungry soul
        Unto the place of vision clear.
How wonderful amid this hush divine,
        Entranced, God's beauty to behold;
To wait whilst deep with deep doth meet and merge,
        And love its secrets doth unfold.
O blessed heights of fellowship with God
        Where love creative reigns supreme,
And springs of never-failing healing rise,
        To gladden, strengthen, and redeem.
                                        —E. C. W. Boulton.

This voice which came from heaven we heard, when we were with him in the holy mount (2 Peter 1:18).

The Secret
of Radiance

They looked unto him, and were lightened (Psa. 34:5).

And all . . . saw his face as it had been the face of an angel (Acts 6:15).

O my soul, wouldest thou have thy life glorified, beautified, transfigured to the eyes of men? Get thee up into the secret place of God's pavilion, where fires of love are burning. Thy life shall shine gloriously to the dwellers on the plain. Thy prayers shall be luminous; they shall light thy face like the face of Moses when he wist it not.—George Matheson.

No human being has ever lived the life of familiarity with the secret place without bearing the light and glory of it on the face. Those who know what it is to talk often with God gain a tone in their talking with men which cannot be mistaken. Herein the subjective value of prayer, but it came out of profound conviction that when they spoke they were heard, when they asked they were answered. I believe, therefore, that the demonstration of the subjective value of prayer is presumptive evidence of its objective value.—G. Campbell Morgan.

> Then only hath the prophet's face
> Put off each weak and human trace,
>   And like an angel's shone;
> When he from crowded camp hath fled,
> And on the mountain summit dread,
> With clouds and darkness overspread,
>   Communed with God alone.
>   —G. Howland.

A spare half hour spent in skimming highly-spiced spiritual literature will never do in the place of gazing in secret upon the Face of our Beloved. "God talked with Moses face to face as a man talketh with his friend." No wonder that his face shone. . . . To have stood thus in the near gaze of God gives a man a tremendous power, and invests the Christian with an awful atmosphere of God, but such transfiguration belongs to none but the lonely seer of the night. For the seer of the unseen is the only true seer. . . . The best seers, not the best sayers, are God's most effectual messengers.—Charles Fox.

It was in a little wood in early morning. The sun was climbing up behind a steep cliff on the east, and its light was flooding nearer and nearer and then making pools among the trees. Suddenly, from a dark corner of purple-brown stems and fawning moss, there shone out a great golden star. It was just a dandelion and half withered, but it was full face to the sun, and had caught into its heart all the glory it could hold, and was shining so radiantly that the dew that lay on it still made a perfect aureole round its head.

If the Sun of Righteousness has risen upon our hearts, there is an ocean of grace and love and power lying all around us, and it is ready to transfigure us, as the sunshine transfigured the dandelion, and on the same condition—that we stand full face to God. Turn your soul's vision to Jesus and look and look at Him, and the Divine attrait by which God's saints are made even in this twentieth century will lay hold of you.—Lillias Trotter.

> Looking upward full of grace,
> He prayed, and from a happy place
> God's glory smote him on the face.
>   —Rev. David Wright, M.A.

I had the particular privilege, when a schoolboy, to come into close contact with Dr. Andrew Bonar. When I was deeply anxious about my soul, I sometimes went to see that beloved saint of God, and there was an atmosphere about him that helped me, even when words did not quite reach the spot.

He kept a diary, never intended for publication, and written in a rather special shorthand, and it would never have seen the light if it had not been that one of his daughters knew this shorthand. In that diary he wrote one day: "Some people have got the beauty of the Rose of Sharon, and there are others who have the fragrance, too. Spent two hours today in prayer, seeking that I might have the fragrance."—W. B. Sloan.

Saturating Our Minds with Christ

Because he hath set his love upon me, therefore will I deliver him: I will set him on high, because he hath known my name. He shall call upon me, and I will answer him (Psa. 91:14, 15).

I am continually with thee: thou hast holden me by my right hand (Psa. 73:23).

While a daily devotional hour is vital for saturating our minds with Christ, it is not enough. All during the day, in the chinks of time between the things we find ourselves obliged to do, there are moments when our minds ask: "What next?" In these chinks of time, ask Him: "Lord, think Thy thoughts in my mind. What is on Thy mind for me to do now?"

When we ask Christ, "What next?" we tune in and give Him a chance to pour His ideas through our enkindled imagination. If we persist, it becomes a habit. It takes some effort, but it is worth a million times what it costs. It is possible for everybody, everywhere. Even if we are surrounded by throngs of people we can continue to talk silently with our invisible Friend. We need not close our eyes nor change our position nor move our lips.

Thinking about Christ constantly is easy to understand. It is not easy to do. Yet there is a way to do it without stopping our other occupations. It is to acquire a new way of thinking. Thinking is a process of talking to your "inner self." Instead of talking to yourself, talk to the invisible Christ.—Frank Laubach.

I am convinced that living in the spirit of prayer from hour to hour is what brings down the blessing.—A. Bonar.

I live in the spirit of prayer. I pray as I walk, when I lie down, and when I arise. The answers are always coming. Thousands and ten

74

thousands of times have my prayers been answered. When once I am persuaded a thing is right, I go on praying for it until the answer comes.
—George Müller.

A continual desire is a continual prayer—that is, in a low sense of the word, for there is a far higher sense, such an open intercourse with God, such a close, uninterrupted communion with Him, as Gregory Lopez experienced, and not a few of our brethren and sisters now alive.—John Wesley.

The prayers of upright Christians are without ceasing; though they pray not always with their mouth, yet their hearts do pray continually; for the sigh of a true Christian is prayer.—Martin Luther.

To the man who never prays . . . there is little hope that a convincing religious experience will ever come. But to the man who prays habitually (not only when he feels like it—that is one of the snares of religion—but also when he does not feel like it) Christ is sure to make Himself real.—James Stewart.

"I am all weakness," wrote William Bramwell in his diary, "indeed, I see nothing will do but a continual dependence and a living upon His mercy—and O the depth of mercy! It is continual prayer that brings the soul into all the glory. . . . I am striving with continual prayer to live nearer to God than I have ever done; and He brings my soul into closer union. I live with Jesus: He is my all. O, He lays me at His feet! I am less than nothing in His sight."

The above breathing of the soul in continuous prayer was the great secret of the success which William Bramwell enjoyed in his changing ministry in Methodism. "He walked in the spirit of believing prayer; acknowledged the hand of God in all things; earnestly sought Divine direction; and daily proved the faithfulness of God. . . . He read, studied, prayed, conversed, groaned in spirit, and most intensely labored for souls." So wrote his biographer.

Familiarity with the Court of Heaven

Did not our heart burn within us, while he talked with us by the way, and while he opened to us the scriptures? (Luke 24:32).

God is faithful, by whom ye were called unto the fellowship of his Son Jesus Christ our Lord (1 Cor. 1:9).

The mercy-seat has a virtue beyond all estimate; the more familiar you are with the court of Heaven the better shall you discharge your heavenly trust. Among all the formative influences which go to make up a man honored of God in the ministry, I know of none more mighty than his own familiarity with the mercy-seat. All that a college course can do for a student is coarse and external compared with the spiritual and delicate refinement obtained by communion with God. While the unformed minister is revolving upon the wheel of preparation, prayer is the tool of the great Potter by which He molds the vessel. All our libraries and studies are mere emptiness compared with our closets. We grow, we wax mighty, we prevail in private prayer.

If you can dip your pens into your hearts, appealing in earnestness to the Lord, you will write well: and if you can gather your matter on your knees at the gate of Heaven, you will not fail to speak well. Prayer, as a mental exercise, will bring many subjects before the mind, and so help the selection of a topic, while as a high spiritual engagement it will cleanse your inner eye that you may see truth in the light of God.

As fresh springs of thought will frequently break up during preparation in answer to prayer, so will it be in the delivery of the sermon. Most preachers who depend upon God's Spirit will tell you that their freshest and best thoughts are not those which were premeditated, but ideas which come to them, flying as on the wings of angels; unexpected treasures brought on a sudden by celestial hands, seeds of the flowers of paradise, wafted from the mountains of myrrh. Often and often when I have felt hampered, both in thought and expression, my secret groaning of heart has brought me relief, and I have enjoyed more than usual liberty. But how dare we pray in the battle if we have never cried to the Lord while buckling on the harness! The remembrance of his wrestlings at home comforts the fettered preacher when in the pulpit: God will not desert us unless we have deserted Him. You, brethren, will find that prayer will ensure you strength equal to your day.—C. H. Spurgeon.

Dr. Theodore Cuyler tells of a visit to Spurgeon's study: "Supper was over; it was Saturday night, and he was going to get his sermon ready. He said, 'Brother, we will have worship now.' He was in awful pain, for his neuralgia was tormenting him. So lame was he that he did not even kneel, but sat at the end of the table. After I had prayed, he just dropped his face between his hands, and began. He talked with God marvelously. He was as simple and as sweet as a child at its mother's knee. He went on, and on, and on. When he had finished, I said to Newman Hall, 'Did you ever hear such a prayer in your life?' 'Never,' he said, 'never.' Said I, 'Now you have the secret of Spurgeon's power. A man who can pray like that can outpreach the world.'"

Forbes Robinson writing to a friend exhorts: "You must force yourself to be alone and to pray. Do make a point of this. You may be eloquent and attractive in your life, but your real effectiveness depends on your communion with the eternal world. You will easily find excuses. Work is so pressing and work is necessary. Other engagements take time. You are tired. You want to go to bed. You go to bed late and want to get up late. So simple prayer and devotion are crowded out. And yet, the necessity is paramount, is inexorable. If you and I are ever to be of any good, if we are to be a blessing, not a curse, to those with whom we are connected, we must enter into ourselves, we must be alone with the only source of unselfishness. If we are of use to others, it will chiefly be because we are simple, pure, unselfish."

Exit All but God

But Peter put them all forth, and kneeled down, and prayed (Acts 9:40).

He went in therefore, and shut the door upon them twain, and prayed unto the LORD (2 Kings 4:33).

Sometimes I wonder if our devotions are not the greatest barrier to spiritual growth, because they are so often just one-sided—it is our praying, it is our talking, our Bible study, our effort. How long is it since you really sat down with great delight in His presence and were conscious that He was flooding your heart and speaking with you?

Some time ago, I was very convicted about this. How often in devotional life, when I was entering into a quiet time, there was the pressure of things and the multitude of thoughts crowding in that can so easily wreck a quiet time. Do you know what I did?

In my room I saw a lot of magazines. I took hold of them and threw them all out. I saw the radio in a corner. I took it and turned it out of the room. Then I saw some books. I shifted them out of the way with some other things. In fact, I just emptied the room of everything that could possibly hinder my thought.

Then I remembered that in the kitchen there were two goldfish in a bowl. I went and brought them into the room. Sitting down on a chair, I watched those goldfish as they leisurely swam round the bowl. They had no sense of concern or anxiety. I concentrated on those goldfish until all the noise and turmoil of Christian service and battle had died down. Then I turned my eyes upon Jesus and looked full in His wonderful face.

I have found that one of the greatest difficulties in the Christian life is to be silent before God, to be still, to sink into nothingness, to stop the rush and the business of life until Jesus Christ gets a chance to speak to the heart.—Alan Redpath.

If we could only be still—
If we could silence the voices of earth and of life—
Voices of discord and strife—
If we could break all these fetters, stand free and alone—
Only God's life and our own,
Then would He make Himself known!
Doth He not fill,
Heaven and earth with His presence, and is He not here,
Speaking and touching? Yet we,
Busy and earth-bound, fail often to hear, and to see
God, the Eternal, so near.
Life is too full of its claims, and earth asks for too much—
Giving too little to quench the one thirst of the heart.
Let us get into the silence, alone and apart—
Hushed for the sound of His voice,
Yes! and calm for His touch.
There we shall look on the Real!
God will reveal
Spirit to spirit—Himself, as He is, unto us—
Claiming the kingdom within us, and filling it thus.

—Edith Hickman Divall.

In a world where there is so much to ruffle the spirit's plumes, how needful that entering into the secret of God's pavilion, which will alone bring it back to composure and peace! In a world where there is so much to sadden and depress, how blessed the communion with Him in Whom is the one true source and fountain of all true gladness and abiding joy! In a world where there is so much to unhallow our spirits, to render them common and profane, how high the privilege of consecrating them anew in prayer.—Trench.

Listening
Pays Well

Blessed are they that hear the word of God (Luke 11:28).

Blessed is the man that heareth me, watching daily at my gates, waiting at the posts of my doors (Prov. 8:34).

A steamship company wanted a wireless operator, and applicants were told to report to the office at a certain time for interview. Several men applied at the stated time, and while waiting in the office they filled the room with such a buzz of conversation that none of them noticed a series of dots and dashes coming over a loudspeaker in the room.

One man, however, who had only just come in and was sitting down by himself, suddenly jumped up and walked into the private office. In a few minutes he came out smiling broadly. He had gotten the job.

"I say," called out one of the men who had been waiting some time, "how did you get in ahead of us? We were here first."

"One of you would have gotten the job," he replied, "if you'd listened to the message on the loudspeaker."

"What message?" they asked in chorus.

"Why, didn't you hear it?" he answered. "It came out in Morse. 'The man I need must be always on the alert. The first man who gets this message and comes directly to my private office will be placed on one of my ships as a wireless operator.'"

When we read the above, we thought of the many Christians, awaiting the coming of the Lord, but so engrossed in idle chatter and the mad rush for material gain that they do not catch the whispers of the Spirit. The early Church had ears which were acutely tuned to the infinite Voice. It told them where to go and when to go, and when obeyed it always paid in souls being truly reached with the right message at the right time.

Let me listen in the quiet
    To the hallowed voice of God,
Nor rising up to follow
    Till my inner feet are shod
In accordance with the Guidebook
    For my ways—His precious Word,
Shutting out all other voices
    That would clamor to be heard.
Let me listen in the quiet
    While His loving hand outpours
All I need, and goes before me
    Opening—and closing—doors!
       —Alice Hansche Mortenson.

There is hardly ever a complete silence in our soul. God is whispering to us well-nigh incessantly. Whenever the sounds of the world die out in the soul . . . then we hear these whisperings of God. He is always whispering to us, only we do not always hear because of the noise, hurry, and distraction which life causes as it rushes on.—F. W. Faber.

Take heed therefore how ye hear (Luke 8:18).

We all know that to do things is easier for most people than to be still. Our lives are like the ocean in their restlessness. This is one of the proofs of our immortality. We are too great to be quiet. A stone has no trouble in keeping still. A clam never gets nervous.

The human soul was made for God, and its very grandeur renders its repose and quiet amid the things of earth the most difficult of all attainments. Yet quietness is a lesson that is set for us with great frequency in the Bible. We are told that the effect of righteousness is quietness. The Shepherd leads His sheep by the still waters. Restlessness is not spiritually beautiful. . . .

Quietness in a man or a woman is a mark of strength. Noise is not eloquence. Loudness is not power. In all departments of life it is the quiet forces that effect most. Therefore, if we would be strong, we must learn to be quiet. Quietness can never come through the hushing of the world's noise so that there shall be nothing to try or irritate the spirit. The quietness must be within us. Nothing but the peace of God in the heart can give it. Yet we can have this peace if we will simply and always do God's will and then trust Him. A quiet heart will give a quiet life.—J. R. Miller.

First Thoughts for God

In the morning shall my prayer prevent (come before) thee (Psa. 88:13).

In the morning the dew lay round about (Exodus 16:13).

His compassions fail not. They are new every morning: great is thy faithfulness (Lam. 3:22, 23).

The best time to converse with God is before worldly occasions stand knocking at the door to be let in: the morning is, as it were, the cream of the day; let the cream be taken off, and let God have it. Wind up thy heart towards Heaven in the beginning of the day, and it will go the better all the day after. He that loseth his heart in the morning in the world, will hardly find it again all the day.

O Christians, let God have your morning meditations! He takes it in disdain to have the world served before Him. Suppose a king and a yeoman were to dine in the same room, and to sit at two tables; if the yeoman should have his meal brought up, and be served first, the king might take it in high disdain, and look upon it as a contempt done to his person. When the world shall be served first, all our morning thoughts attending it, and the Lord shall be put off with the dregs of the day, is not this a contempt done to the God of glory?

God deserves the first of our thoughts; some of His first thoughts were upon us; we had a being in His thoughts before we had a being; He thought upon us "before the foundations of the world." Before we fell He was thinking how to raise us. We had the morning of His thoughts. We have taken up His thoughts from eternity: if we have had some of God's first thoughts, well may He have our first thoughts. In the morning the dew fell (Exod. 16:13). The dew of a blessing falls early; now we are likeliest to have God's company. If you would meet with a friend, you go betimes in the morning before he be gone out.—T. Watson.

Begin each fresh and new-born day with God
Before its unknown pathway has been trod;
Before the calls of duty loudly sound,
And hours with busy moments hurry round.
Kneel down and humbly offer up your prayer
In sweet communion with the Lord, and share
With Him the joy of fellowship and love
Born of that union with His life above.
Then read and meditate upon His Word,
Till faith is quickened and your soul is stirred.
If thus you seek a vision of His Face,
And learn still more of His abounding grace,
All through the day God's peace will then abide
Within your heart, and every step He'll guide.
—F. D. Walker.

The building of one of our modern cathedrals had taken a long time, and the work had been very wearisome. Added to this, there was a particularly irritating foreman in charge. And there was a considerable amount of grumbling among the men. That is—all except one man, a cement mixer, whose job was monotonous. But he always seemed to be whistling happily.

On a very wet and miserable day, someone asked him how he could whistle while the others were so gloomy.

"Well," he replied, "every morning before I start, I pop into the works office and look at the picture of the finished cathedral hanging on the wall, and I think what a grand job we're on, and I realize that even I, though just a mortar mixer, am playing a part in a great work—building a great cathedral which will stand here one day."—Harold Tweedie.

All through life, like Wesley, George Whitefield was an early-riser. His day began at four o'clock all the year round, and he would retire just as punctually at ten in the evening. If any company were present he would cut proceedings short very courteously with "Come, gentlemen! It is time for all good folks to be at home." He was punctuality incarnate, being as careful of other people's time as of his own. The test of popularity is one of the fiercest a man can endure, and from the age of twenty-one to his life's end Whitefield stood that test well.—A. D. Belden.

Dew
or Do

I will be as the dew unto Israel: he shall grow as the lily, and cast forth his roots as Lebanon. His branches shall spread, and his beauty shall be as the olive tree (Hos. 14:5, 6).

The heavens shall give their dew (Zech. 8:12).

When God's judgment fell upon Israel of old, it began with the loss of the finer things. How true this still is. Long before a backslider comes out into the open and flings aside his faith and service, a fearful thing has taken place—the "dew has been stayed." Knowledge remains, the old terms are used, service is still engaged in, but it is hollow, brassy, powerless. We look in vain for those finer spiritual qualities that contribute that spiritual power that touches the deepest springs of the human heart.

The dew, we are told, falls in the still night when all nature is hushed to rest. What is true in nature is true in spiritual things. In this we have the key to the reason why so many of God's people are living dewless lives. They are restless, anxious, impatient, fussy, busy, with no time to be still before the Lord. The finer things are being sacrificed for the coarser, the things of value for the worthless, the things that matter for those of no value. It is in the stillness that He gives His finest things. Seek the dew-drenched life that is always fresh and fragrant.

Men are eagerly, feverishly rushing after their own things. Prayer is a lost art; communion and meditation that transformed the lives of the saints in the past are now spoken of as mystical and impractical. Beware of sacrificing the dew of your spiritual life for the wealth, pleasure, and popularity of this passing age. Retain, even at the price of sacrifice, the finer spiritual qualities that make life's ministries mighty.

In Numbers 11:9 we learn that the manna fell upon the dew. The food of the mighty (Psa. 78:25, margin), the corn of heaven (Psa. 78:24), was given in the stillness. This is the secret of spiritual health. Wait on the Lord, and as you wait He will feed you with that which makes men mighty. Seek the dew-drenched food. "My speech shall distil as the dew" (Deut. 32:2). Words that fall upon the ear in the stillness are distilled again as the dew on needy lives around us.

"The remnant of Jacob shall be in the midst of many people as a dew from the LORD" (Mic. 5:7). Not only are we to be dew-drenched ourselves, but we are to be as the dew of the Lord to others. Our lives may exercise that quiet, hidden influence that refreshes and strengthens the weary lives around us.

Hosea 14:5 leads us to the source of this dew-drenched life: "I will be as the dew." It is from Him this priceless gift comes. Those who spend much time with the Master come forth with the dew of blessing upon their lives.

In Job 38:28 the question is asked: "Who hath begotten the drops of dew?" It is one of God's secrets. It comes quietly, noiselessly, and yet works so mightily. We cannot produce it, but we may receive it and live moment by moment in that atmosphere where the Holy Spirit may continually drench us with His presence. What the dew is to the earth, so the Holy Spirit longs to be to us—a daily refreshing of new life, new strength, rare beauty, and fragrance.—W. Mallis.

> God's spirit falls on me as dew drops on a rose,
> If I but like a rose my heart to Him unclose.
> —Johannes Scheffler.

I see that unless I keep up short prayer every day throughout the whole day, at intervals, I lose the spirit of prayer. Too much work without corresponding prayer. Today—setting myself to pray. The Lord forthwith seems to send a dew upon my soul. Passed six hours today in prayer and Scripture-reading, confessing sin, and seeking blessing for myself and the parish.—Andrew Bonar.

Intercessory Participation

To the weak became I as weak, that I might gain the weak: I am made all things to all men, that I might by all means save some. And this I do for the gospel's sake, that I might be partaker thereof with you (1 Cor. 9:22, 23).

I sat where they sat (Ezek. 3:15).

A dear friend of mine was sick and was seemingly nigh unto death. I was much in prayer for him that he might be spared to his family and to his friends and to his great work. One night as I was in that intercessory prayer a voice suddenly spake and said to me, "Are you in real earnest in what you ask? Or are you uttering, as usual, so many of your idle words in this solemn matter? Now to prove the sincerity and the integrity of your love for your friend, and to seal the truth of what you say about the value of his life, will you give Me and yourself a solid proof that you are in real earnest in what you say?"

"What is the proof?" I asked, all trembling and without looking up.

The voice said, "Will you consent to transfer to your sick friend the half of your remaining years? Suppose you have two more years to live and work for yourself. Will you give over one of them to your friend? Or if you have ten years yet before you, will you let your friend have five of them?"

I sprang to my feet in a torrent of sweat. It was a kind of garden of Gethsemane to me. But, like Gethsemane, I got strength to say, "Let it be as Thou hast said. Thy will be done. Not my will but Thine be done." I lay down that never-to-be-forgotten night with a clean heart and a good conscience as never before, both toward God and toward my much-talented friend.

How the matter is to end, I know not. How the case is to work out, I cannot tell. Enough for me and for you that my story is true and is no idle tale.—Alexander Whyte.

Rees Howells, before he became founder of the Bible College of Wales, was being prepared for larger intercessory service. He found his heart going out in prayer for the drunkards in his neighborhood. He felt he could only pray aright if he entered somewhat into their state, and so he denied himself of the food that would normally have been his and took the bread, cheese, and soup that he knew was the daily portion of these men reduced in circumstances through alcohol.

Mathilde Wrede, Baroness Wrede, became known as "The Angel of the Prisons." At twenty, this former gay, rich young woman was called by God to labor among the prisoners of Finland. In her home she lived on the same fare as the prisoners and they knew it and loved her for it. One morning, several Bolsheviks came to ask money of her. "Money I have, but it is for the old and sick." They pleaded hunger and so she said they might share her breakfast. It was but a single slice of bread and cabbage. She apologized and invited them back to tea when she said something more substantial would be prepared for them.

In a very small way these people learned something of what it meant for Jesus to leave the glories of Heaven to come to our sin-stricken world, and that He might be able to experience all the points in which we were to be tempted and so be able to succor us in His eternal intercession at the Father's right hand.

> But Lord, this ceaseless travail of my soul,
> This stress, this often fruitless toil, these souls to win—
>   They are not mine;
> I brought not forth this host
> Of needy creatures, struggling, tempest-tossed—
>   They are not mine.
> He looked at them, the look of one divine—
> He turned and looked at me:
>   **"But they are Mine."**
> O God, I said, I understand at last.
> Forgive! and henceforth I will bond-slave be
> To Thy least, weakest, vilest ones:
> I would no more be free! He smiled and said,
>   **"It is to Me."**
>   —Unknown.

Fellowship of
the Pierced Hand

I . . . fill up that which is behind of the afflictions of Christ (Col. 1:23,24).

Jesus . . . groaned in the spirit, and was troubled (John 11:33).

Jesus therefore again groaning in himself cometh to the grave (John 11:38).

I do not know how any Christian service is to be fruitful if the servant is not primarily baptized in the Spirit of a suffering compassion. We can never heal the needs we do not feel. Tearless hearts can never be the heralds of the Passion. We must pity if we would redeem. We must bleed if we would be the ministers of the saving blood. We must perfect by our passion the Passion of the Lord, and by our suffering sympathies we must "fill up that which is behind" in the sufferings of Christ.

If the prayer of the disciple is to fill up the intercession of the Master, the disciple's prayer must be stricken with much crying and many tears. The ministers of Calvary must supplicate in bloody sweat, and their intercession must often touch the point of agony. If we pray in cold blood, we are no longer the ministers of the cross. True intercession is a sacrifice, a perpetuation of Calvary, a filling up of the sufferings of Christ.

My brethren, this is the ministry which the Master owns, the agonized yearnings which perfect the sufferings of His own intercession. Are we in the succession? Do our prayers bleed? Have we felt the painful fellowship of the pierced hand? I am often ashamed of my prayers. They so frequently cost me nothing; they shed no blood. I am amazed at the grace and condescension of my Lord that He confers any fruitfulness upon my superficial pains.

To be, therefore, in the sacrificial succession, our sympathy must be a passion, our intercession must be a groaning, our beneficence must be a sacrifice, and our service must be a martyrdom. In everything there must be the shedding of blood.

How can we attain unto it? What is the secret of the sacrificial life? It is here. The men and women who willingly and joyfully share the fellowship of Christ's sufferings are vividly conscious of the unspeakable reality of their own personal redemption. They never forget the pit out of which they have been digged, and they never lose the remembrance of the grace that saved them. He "loved me, and gave himself for me" (Gal. 2:20). Therefore, I "glory in tribulations" (Rom. 5:3). "By the grace of God I am what I am" (1 Cor. 15:10). Therefore "I will very gladly spend and be spent" (2 Cor. 12:15).

—J. H. Jowett.

Oh, for a passionate passion for souls!
    Oh, for a pity that yearns!
Oh, for the love that loves unto death!
    Oh, for the fire that burns!
Oh, for the pure prayer-power that prevails,
    That pours itself out for the lost—
Victorious prayer in the Conqueror's name;
    Oh, for a Pentecost!

Infinite Savior, in mighty compassion,
    Take Thy poor child tonight;
That which she hath not, in tenderness give.
    Teach her to pray and to fight.
Cost what it may, of a self-crucifixion,
    So that Thy will be done:
Cost what it may, of a loneliness after,
    So only souls be won.
                    —Amy Carmichael.

The Divinity of Groans

My groaning is not hid from thee (Psa. 38:9).

God heard their groaning, and God remembered (Exodus. 2:24).

Christ receives sighs in His censer for prayers; though others mock at groans, yet He that made them knows what they mean. The Spirit that made them knows what they mean. The Spirit first makes the sigh as an intercessor, and then as God hears it, He is within praying, and without hearing. A dumb beggar gets an alms at Christ's gate, even by making signs. The Lord regards not the grammar of prayers, how men word it in prayer; nor the arithmetic of prayers, how often they pray; nor the rhetoric of prayer, how finely they pray; nor the music of prayer, what sweetness of tone men have in prayer; but the divinity of groans. There are sighs and groans which cannot be uttered.—Francis Raworth.

A burning Niagara of words does not mean that God is either impressed or moved. Hannah, the mother of Samuel, one of the most pro-found of intercessors, had no language. "Her lips moved, but her voice was not heard." There are groanings that cannot be uttered. In the mountain-moving place of travailing prayer, linguists are not needed.—L. Ravenhill.

Mental prayer is not unheard—"Hannah spake in her heart." When the heart is so full of grief that it can only groan in prayer, yet God writes that down: "My groaning is not hid from Thee."—Watson.

Though smooth be the heartless prayer,
No ear in Heaven will mind it,
And the finest phrase falls dead,
If there is no feeling behind it.

So it is not the speech which tells,
>But the impulse which goes with the saying,
And it is not the words of the prayer,
>But the yearning back of the praying.
>>—E. W. Wilcox.

"Groanings which cannot be uttered" are often prayers which cannot be refused.—C. H. Spurgeon.

One of the most used evangelists in the revivals which stirred the churches in the 1840's and added many thousands to the different denominations, the Rev. James Caughey, who had the unspeakable privilege of leading General Booth to the Savior, labored fervently for the sanctification of believers in all his campaigns. He was one of the most used, but most maligned evangelists of that period. To read his letters is both an education and inspiration. In one of them he says:

"The power of the Holy Ghost accompanying hard, patient, steady, constant labor with many tears, and much crying to God in private have produced the results which seem so mysterious to you. Knee work! Knee work! This is the secret.

>"'My powerful groans thou canst not bear,
>Nor stand the violence of prayer,
>>My prayer omnipotent.'

"'Give me a revival, convert sinners, or I pine away and die,' is the cry that is much thought of in Heaven; nor will He who pities the groanings of the distressed soul, treat it with indifference. He will come down out of His holy place and make bare His arm in the sight of the people, wound the dragon, and cut Rahab in pieces. Then shall the feeblest servant of God often thresh the mountains, and beat the hills to chaff; one shall chase a thousand and two shall put ten thousand to flight, and the slain of the Lord shall be many.

"Let any minister thus plead with God, while week after week, every night from a full and bleeding heart, he pours the burning, pointed truths of the Gospel into the ranks of sinners and whatever may be his talents, he shall be a joyful witness of a glorious revival. This is the secret philosophy of revivals."

Prayer that Moves Heaven

*Their cry came up unto God. . . . And God heard their groaning. . . .
And God looked upon the children of Israel, and God had respect
unto them (Exodus 2:23-25).*

*Now therefore, behold, the cry of the children of Israel is come
unto me: and I have also seen the oppression (Exodus 3:9).*

Heaven is not moved by oratory, but it will be moved by soul
agony and tears. There is much that ought to cause us agony of soul
these days. . . . For instance, the Church's apostasy and ineffectiveness
and the world's indifference and wickedness; and the latter because
of the former for the Church is the light and the salt in a dark and
corrupt world, so that if the light be darkness and the salt have lost its
savor what hope is there for a poor fallen world? It is useless to rail
the world's indifference if our hearts are not moved with compassion
over the shepherdless sheep.

The need of the day is men and women who can pray; those who
feel acutely the present situation, and who are under the burden of the
world's need to such an extent that it is no self-inflicted penance to
fast and pray and absent themselves from the social circle until their
burden is lifted and deliverance is come.

Many are afraid to allow God to bring them into a prayer life
such as is described above: it costs too much; it may cut the life short,
and will most certainly bring misunderstanding and misrepresentation
for such lives of prayer are very rare, so rare, that when God calls men
and women into such a fellowship with Himself they are often looked
upon as eccentric.—Stanley Banks.

Hyde paid a price for such prayer. Often he was ranked as a mad
enthusiast, and considered as one who went much too far. He also
paid the price in a shortened life for such agonizing prayer. But he
has left a fragrance of life behind him that whenever the name is

mentioned, we smell the sweetness of a life poured out before God for men.—H.

There is no power like that of prevailing prayer—of Abraham pleading for Sodom, Jacob wrestling in the stillness of the night, Moses standing in the breach, Hannah intoxicated with sorrow, David heartbroken with remorse and grief, Jesus in sweat of blood.

Add to this list from the records of the church—your personal observation and experience, and always there is the cost of passion unto blood. Such prayer prevails. It turns ordinary mortals into men of power. It brings life. It brings God.*—Samuel Chadwick.

> Stir me, oh stir me, Lord, I care not how,
>   But stir my heart in passion for the world!
> Stir me to give, to go—but most to pray,
>   Stir 'til the blood-red banner be unfurled
> O'er lands that still in heathen darkness lie,
> Lands where the cross was never lifted high.
>
> Stir me! oh stir me, Lord, 'til all my heart
>   Is filled with strong compassion for these souls,
> 'Til that compelling "must" drives me to pray,
>   'Til Thy constraining love reach to the poles,
> Far north and south, in burning deep desire,
> 'Til east and west are caught in love's great fire.
>   —Mrs. H. Head.

When Christmas Evans was once on his travels between Dolgelly and Machynlleth he had such a view of God's glory that he felt that the barren mountain of Cader Idris had become a Holy of Holies. He wrestled with God for several hours, praying for the churches and ministers of Wales by name. What wonder that he returned to Anglesey like a giant refreshed, and that a strong religious awakening was the natural result!

*From *The Path of Prayer* by Samuel Chadwick. (London: Hodder & Stoughton). Copyright 1931 by Samuel Chadwick. Copyright 1956 by Hodder and Stoughton Limited.

The
Marked Ones

And the LORD said unto him . . . Set a mark upon the foreheads of the men that sigh and that cry for all the abominations that be done . . . and begin at my sanctuary (Ezek. 9:4, 6).

They have not cried unto me with their heart (Hosea 7:14).

The marked ones are those who, having trusted Jesus Christ for complete deliverance from the dominion of sin, have a heart to sympathize with Him in His sorrow over a world redeemed by His precious blood, yet "lying in the lap of the evil one." Many Christians spend their time in sighing and crying over their own sins and inconsistencies, and have no power to exercise their priestly function of intercession for others. To all such Jesus says, "Come unto Me with that which wearies you and burdens you, and I will give you rest; then take My yoke upon you and learn of Me." In other words, "Bring your burdens to Me: I alone have power to remove them; and having freed you from your burdens, I will transfer My burden to you, and give you to know something of the fellowship of My sufferings."

Oh, for a host of men and women who are thus freed to sigh and cry over these things that grieve the heart of Jesus and retard the coming of His kingdom!

When Mrs. McAulay went to toil in the East of London with her devoted husband, she was so heartbroken at what she saw of the ravages of sin and the impotence of the Christian Church that she cried herself blind. The sight of one eye was restored, but she carried one sightless eye to her grave, thus bearing in her body the marks of the Lord Jesus. She knew, indeed, what it was to sigh and cry over the abominations done in the city.

Matthew Henry thinks that because this was a mark which the Lord Jesus alone could give, a heart-designation which only He could adjudge, the man clothed in linen, was no other than He. The identity of this messenger is of little importance; what is important is that, whether we lie in the sick chamber and have weary days and nights appointed to us, whether it is ours to be in the front of the battle, to watch by the campfire, or to guard the stuff, we have the mark of God upon our forehead, which a well-known writer interprets as the putting of His character upon our character.—J. Gregory Mantle.

"He continued in prayer to God." "And as he prayed his sweat was as it were great drops of blood." Has our season of prayer any resemblance to these? Does it suggest energy and sacrifice, even to the point of blood? Are our intercessions weighted with purpose, and have we the demeanor of an armed man cleaving his way to some shining palace of gold?

How much do we put into it? Many of us have scarcely begun to pray at all.

We have only played at praying. It has not been a mighty business; it has only been a harmless convention. We have put nothing into it, and therefore we have taken nothing out. We have "prayed amiss."

—J. H. Jowett.

He loved men's souls. Upon his brow
The light of Heaven sat. His lips
Were touched with "coal from off the altar,"
And ever spake the message of his God.
And on his heart he bare the Church
For whom Christ died. And when the dark
Had softly veiled the earth, and men
In slumber sank, he wrestled for their souls,
And in affliction sore, and many tears,
He kept the watch alone with God.

—Unknown.

Travail
Brings Birth

My little children, of whom I travail in birth again until Christ be formed in you (Gal. 4:19).

Ye remember, brethren, our labour and travail (1 Thess. 2:9).

The birth of a natural child is pre-dated by months of burden and days of travail; so is the birth of a spiritual child. Jesus prayed for His Church but then to bring it to spiritual birth He **gave** Himself in death. Paul prayed "night and day . . . exceedingly" for the Church; moreover, he travailed for the sinners. It was "when Zion travailed, that she brought forth."

Though preachers each week cry, "Ye must be born again," how many could say with Paul, "Though ye have ten thousand instructors in Christ, yet have ye not many fathers: for in Christ Jesus **I have begotten** you through the gospel"? So he fathered them in the faith. He does not say that he merely prayed for them; he implies that he **travailed** for them.

In the past century, if the physical birth rate had been as low as the spiritual birth rate, the human race would now be almost extinct. "We must pray to live the Christian life," we say; whereas the truth is that we must live the Christian life to pray. "If ye abide . . . ye shall ask" (i.e., pray). I know that "asking" includes making our requests for the salvation of loved ones, but prayer is more than asking. Prayer, surely, is getting us into subjection to the Holy Ghost so that He can work in and through us. In the first chapter of Genesis every thing that had life brought forth its kind. Then in regeneration should not every really born-again soul bring others to birth?

Women of the Bible who had been barren brought forth its noblest children: Sarah, barren until ninety years of age, begat Isaac; Rachel's cutting cry, "Give me children, or else I die!" was answered, and she bore Joseph, who delivered the nation. Manoah's wife bare Samson, another deliverer of the nation. Hannah, a smitten soul, after sobbing in the sanctuary and vowing vows and continuing in prayer, ignored Eli's scorn, poured out her soul, and received her answer in Samuel, who became the prophet of Israel. The barren and widowed Ruth found mercy and bare Obed, who begat Jesse, the father of David, of whose line came our Savior. Of Elizabeth, stricken in years, came John the Baptist, of whom Jesus said there was no greater prophet born of women. If shame of childlessness had not subdued these women, what mighty men would have been lost!

It is true that science has alleviated some of the suffering that our mothers knew in childbirth; but science will never shrink the long slow months of child-formation. In the same way we preachers have also found easier methods of getting folk to the altars for salvation or for the filling with the Holy Ghost. For salvation, folk are permitted just to slip up their hand, and, presto! the groaning at the altar is eliminated. For the filling with the Holy Ghost, men are told to "Just stand where you are while the evangelist prays for you, and you will be filled." Oh, the shame of it! Brother, before the miracle takes place, true revival and soul-birth still demand travail.—L. Ravenhill.

"If God," says Maurice, "had not heard this prayer, going up from tens of thousands in all ages, the earth would have been a den of robbers." We do not know from what depths of depravity this pleading, offered continually by loyal hearts, has saved the world. Nor do we begin to realize what Christianity has wrought in the world, in the countries where it has had power.—Miller.

Accomplishment Through Travail

He shall see of the travail of his soul, and shall be satisfied (Isa. 53:11).

Ye remember, brethren, our labour and travail (1 Thess. 2 :9).

We must remember that it was not by interceding for the world in Glory that Jesus saved it. He gave Himself. Our prayers for the evangelization of the world are but a bitter irony so long as we give only of our superfluity, and draw back before the sacrifice of ourselves.
—M. Francois Collard.

Do not think that He accomplished His work through the travailing of His soul to dispense us from having anything to do or to suffer in His cause.

He opened the way that we might follow. Ah! we have yet to learn what it is to travail in birth for souls, till Christ be formed in them. We have yet to learn what the Apostle meant when he said that he filled up what remained of the sufferings of Christ for His body's sake, which is the Church. We have much of outward working, much of organization, much of speaking and hearing, much of publishing and reading; but, I fear, very little of that bearing of the souls of men upon our own souls, in love, in tears, in prayer before God.—T. Monod.

God's greatest gifts to man come through travail. Whether we look into the spiritual or temporal sphere, can we discover anything, any great reform, any beneficent discovery, any soul-awakening revival, which did not come through the toils and tears, the vigils and blood-shedding of men and women whose sufferings were the pangs of its birth?

If the temple is to be raised, David must bear sore afflictions; if the Gospel of the grace of God is to be disentangled from Jewish tradition, Paul's life must be one long agony.—F. B. Meyer.

There is a distinct connection between importunate agonizing and true success, even as between the travail and the birth, the sowing in tears and the reaping in joy. "How is it that your seed comes up so soon?" said one gardener to another. "Because I steep it," was the reply. We must all steep our teachings in tears, "when none but God is nigh," and their growth will surprise and delight us.—Selected.

"Prayer and Pains, with faith in God, can accomplish anything," said John Elliot. Among the early Pilgrim Fathers to go to New England, he had become concerned about the state of the Indians and is called by some The Father of Modern Missions. He was the first to translate the Scriptures into a heathen tongue for missionary purposes but it was by prayer and pains that he endured the arduous task of evangelism. His last exhortation, as he lay dying at the age of 87, to those he left behind, was "Pray, pray, pray," revealing the secret of his own life of service.—H.

Leslie Lyall, in his biography of John Sung, says of his prayer life: "He was undoubtedly a man of prayer. He rose very early in the morning to pray. A well-nigh interminable list of his converts and, if possible, their photographs was his inseparable companion and he prayed for them all regularly, often with tears. Everywhere he went he laid emphasis on the urgent need to pray. That the Chinese Church is a praying Church today can be attributed in part to the influence and the example of this man who prayed. . . . He could never waste a minute."

And when John Sung was about to finish his earthly ministry, his closing message to the Church in China was: "The work of the future is to be the work of prayer!"

Howard Guiness, realizing what an important part prayer ought to play in his missionary endeavors in China, said: "From today the central thing in my life shall be prayer."

How Rare
a Burden

Horror hath taken hold upon me because of the wicked that forsake thy law (Psa 119:53).

The burden which Habakkuk the prophet did see. O LORD, how long shall I cry, and thou wilt not hear! (Hab. 1:1, 2).

A burden is a load of care or sorrow. The most important work of the child of God is intercession. No-one will ever be a winner of souls unless he has the burden of souls. When this burden is on us we do not merely think about souls but we cry to God on their behalf.

It is a serious matter to be without such a burden. This bespeaks lukewarmness, indifference, and the absence of the Holy Spirit from the believer's heart. Many shrink from this burden and well may they, for unless sustained by the power of God no one could stand the strain. Yet withal there are compensations that can only be entered into by such as have felt the pain and sorrow of soul-travail.

In an article, I came across the following statement: "For weeks a burden has rested upon me because of the spiritual barrenness of the churches and ministry, and on behalf of the unsaved. The burden has been very heavy, at times almost unbearable, and has impelled to prayer, even to prolonged seasons. Sometimes in sleep at night prayer has continued all night long in dreams. Presently a depressing fear came that such a state might not be normal, but the beginning of insanity. The distress of mind was carefully concealed from those around me, a sense of utter loneliness fell on the soul, but when the Word was turned to, there were the promises and precedents, as 'The Spirit Himself maketh intercession . . . with groanings which cannot be uttered.'"

Three weeks fasting and agonizing by Daniel; the all night prayers of our Lord; the testimony of Paul—so faith was encouraged. Then came an article by the Editor of the *Sunday School Times* showing that God had been laying a like burden on many Christians. Specially comforting was the statement about the Director of the Great Commission Prayer League—"having an overwhelming, well-nigh intolerable burden." Here was a man having the same kind of experience! Oh, the relief and joy and thankfulness that followed!

Are we to conclude that such examples as we have shown in the preceding paragraphs were men striving after effect and notoriety? Or are we to conclude that the visible effects seen upon them and experienced by them were but outward evidences of some great heart-sorrow or burden?

The great need of the hour is mighty intercessors. If the Church of Christ could lay hold of God in mighty intercession, multitudes that are still on the broad road to destruction could be won for Christ. Oh, that He would pour out upon us the spirit of prayer and supplication.

—J. D. Drysdale.

> Fill me, fill me, create within me
> Love that has a passion for souls,
> Never I needed Thee more than this moment,
> Fill me with Thy Holy Spirit.
> —Unknown.

The pleading, the wrestling, nay, the agonizing element will have to enter more powerfully into our prayers if we would see this great people turning to God. It is very much easier to work than to pray. Most of the missionaries are earnest workers. But are we all that we should be in the matter of prayer? Let us not suppose that any sort of praying will do for China. We must all wrestle with God. "I will not let Thee go unless Thou bless China." It must come to this if the conversion of the Chinese is ever to be an accomplished fact. Such is my conviction.

Let me remind you that the greatest importunity is not incompatible with the profoundest submission to the Divine will.—Griffith John.

The Spirit-Inspired Discontent

Not only they, but ourselves also, which have the firstfruits of the Spirit, even we ourselves groan within ourselves, waiting . . . (Rom. 8:23).

Quench not the Spirit (1 Thess. 5:19).

Grieve not the holy Spirit of God (Eph. 4:30).

As the Spirit interprets the will of God, therefore, He makes the soul profoundly discontented with everything that is contrary thereto, and this because of the soul's supreme content with the "good, and acceptable, and perfect, will of God." That is what the Apostle meant when he wrote, "The whole creation groaneth and travaileth in pain together until now. And not only they, but ourselves also, which have the firstfruits of the Spirit, even we ourselves groan within ourselves." Faber sang this sublime and overwhelming truth in simplest words:

> "There is no place where earth's sorrows
> Are more felt than up in Heaven."

The heavenly people are, therefore, those who most acutely feel earth's sorrows and are able to enter into fellowship with God in prayer for the winning of the victories of His love.

Following consciousness of discontent is that of desire for the coming of the Kingdom, for the setting up of the will of God, which means the healing of wounds and the breaking of chains.

To that work of the indwelling Spirit there must be ready response. "Quench not the Spirit." When the Spirit interprets the will of God for life, for home, for city, for nation, we must listen to no other philosophy, be seduced by no other ideal. As the glories of that Kingdom flame and flash before us, we must never be turned aside by the glamor of the things of the world, the flesh, and the devil. Answer the Spirit. Let Him teach. Let Him show the vision. Believe the Spirit. "Quench not the Spirit."

But more, infinitely more. When the Spirit, revealing the will of God for the world, creates in the heart a great pain and a great discontent, do not let us check it. That is what Christian men and women, alas, are too constantly doing. When the story of the sin and sorrow of humanity is told, they close their ears and are not willing to share in the pain. That is to grieve the Spirit indeed. We ought to hear. We ought to know. We ought to be ready to bring the new sensitiveness of our Christian life into close touch with the world's agony until we feel its pain as our very own. The Spirit desires that we should know its sorrow. His work is to interpret to us the meaning of the sob and sigh and the agony of the world. When we feel that, there will spring out of our life a new desire which will drive us to prayer that God's Kingdom may come, and to self-sacrificing service without which such prayer is blasphemy. Thus we shall begin to sob with God and to God, in our sense of the world's sorrow. Out of such prayer the toil and travail come which bring the Kingdom in.*

—G. Campbell Morgan.

Last night I had a unique experience. I awoke intensely oppressed and as I lay under the dead weight of it, it dawned on me that it meant I was to pray, so I got to work to pray for the men who have just gone off to the fighting line, and in a marvelous way the oppression left and peace ineffable came, and the words emerged, "A house of prayer for all nations." It is a good thing to stake your confidence on the ground of the perfected Redemption and pray from that basis.

—Oswald Chambers.

Pastor Hsi was especially sensitive to the discontent inspired by the Holy Spirit. In the midst of absorbing labor he would become troubled and over-powered with faintness. Though neither rest nor food would relieve him, prayer always did. It usually became clear later that there was some very great need arising somewhere at that very moment.

*From *The Practice of Prayer* by G. Campbell Morgan. (London: Hodder & Stoughton). Copyright 1907 by G. Campbell Morgan.

Prayer Specialists Required

Gehazi . . . laid the staff upon the face of the child; but there was neither voice, nor hearing. . . . He (Elijah) went in therefore, and shut the door upon them twain, and prayed unto the LORD . . . and the child opened his eyes (2 Kings 4:31, 33, 35).

Scientists often spend years, sometimes a whole lifetime, in making important scientific discovery. Then how can we expect to discover spiritual beauties by spending only five minutes every day in quiet and prayer? Some people become tired at the end of ten minutes or half an hour of prayer. What would they do when they have to spend Eternity in the presence of God? We must begin the habit here and become used to being with God.—Sadhu Sundar Singh.

We have, in our world of today, specialists of many different kinds. The marvel is that God does not have more prayer-specialists. The need is so great for such who can find easy access to God and know how to help souls in dire need. Mrs. Peter Marshall was the wife of a Presbyterian clergyman who became chaplain to the United States Senate. While still in his early forties thrombosis struck her husband, and in her dilemma Mrs. Marshall wrote:

"But how many of us, we who had been in churches all our lives, knew how to pray? I did not. Seemingly a thousand times that day I had shut my eyes tight and demanded, 'God, make him well. God, please dissolve that blood clot.' But that was not prayer, and I knew it. Tenseness and fear shut out God and I was afraid, desperately afraid.

"I longed for the help of prayer veterans—people who had not wasted precious time as I had wasted it; people who had disciplined themselves to use ordinary run-of-the-mill days for spiritual research; people who knew why it was that some prayers are answered and some are not; people who were so filled with Christ's presence that they could be relaxed and calm, even in the face of coronary thrombosis. Suddenly, all former values that I had attached to my friends dropped away. I knew wonderful people who were specialists in nearly every field but that of prayer—trained musicians, engineers, lawyers, even doctors. But in a legal crisis, one does not call on an engineer. Faced with an emergency operation one does not want just anybody who means well, but the best surgeon available. Why, then, I reasoned, not apply this same common sense to the art of prayer?"

And Mrs. Marshall did find the help she needed in an elderly, motherly woman, Dr. Beard. She again writes in her book: "She attempted no pat explanation of Peter's death; offered no advice for the future. Sometimes there were tears in her own eyes. Then finally, when the well of my emotion was dry, she said quietly: 'As a doctor, I have only one remedy to offer for what ails you. Let's talk to Christ about it.'

"Her prayer was simple heartfelt claiming of Christ's promise to bind the broken-hearted. Then when she had finished, without another word she gathered me into her ample arms. That afternoon it was as if a gentle hand were laid on my heart. From that moment the healing began somewhere in the depths of my being. As a wound that heals from the inside out, so the restoration was to come, gently.

"I know now that this specific asking for the touch of the Great Physician for my torn emotions was an invaluable step. I also do not believe that that prayer would have had the same effectiveness had it not been made in my presence. Nor can it be as effective if it is a casual prayer, a sort of overflow of goodwill on the part of one's friends. The prayer for the healing of the broken-hearted must be an appointed prayer act—at a definite time and in a definite place. This is the responsibility that persons and Christian friends need to undertake for the sorrowing; they fail us if they do not."

He hath sent me to heal the brokenhearted, to preach deliverance to the captives, and recovering of sight to the blind (Luke 4:18).

The Power of
Life and Death

If any man see his brother sin a sin which to not unto death, he shall ask, and he shall give him life for them that sin not unto death (1 John 5:16).

If we are not heedful of the way the Spirit of God works in us, we shall become spiritual hypocrites. We see where other folks are failing, and we turn our discernment into the gibe of criticism instead of into intercession on their behalf. The revelation is made to us not through the acuteness of our minds but by the direct penetration of the Spirit of God, and if we are not heedful of the source of the revelation, we shall become criticizing centers and forget that God says: ". . . he shall ask, and he shall give him life for them that sin not unto death." Take care lest you play the hypocrite by spending all your time trying to get others right before you worship God yourself.

One of the subtlest burdens God ever puts on us as saints is this burden of discernment concerning other souls. He reveals things in order that we may take the burden of these souls before Him and form the mind of Christ about them, and as we intercede on His line, God says He will give us "life for them that sin not unto death." It is not that we bring God into touch with our minds, but that we rouse ourselves until God is able to convey His mind to us about the one for whom we intercede.

Is Jesus Christ seeing of the travail of His soul in us? He cannot unless we are so identified with Himself that we are roused up to get His view about the people for whom we pray. May we learn to intercede wholeheartedly that Jesus Christ will be abundantly satisfied with us as intercessors.—O. Chambers.

The power of life and death is in our hands (1 John 5:16). In answer to prayer, the Spirit can be poured out, souls can be converted, believers can be established. In prayer, the kingdom of darkness can be conquered, souls brought out of prison into the liberty of Christ, and the glory of God be revealed. Through prayer, the sword of the Spirit, which is the Word of God, can be wielded in power, and, in public preaching as in private speaking, the most rebellious made to bow at Jesus' feet.

What a responsibility on the Church to give herself to the work of intercession!—Andrew Murray.

Pardon, I beseech thee, the iniquity of this people. . . . And the LORD said, I have pardoned (Num. 14:19, 20).

The faculty of discernment is not a gift to be lightly esteemed. It cannot be trifled with. It may be easily obscured or entirely lost, through want of watchfulness or through careless walking. And when lost it is not easily restored. Few gifts are more precious than this faculty of spiritual eyesight, or the sense by which any lowering of the moral temperature may at once be detected. Often it will be the means of keeping us from venturing into scenes where the Spirit of God would be grieved, and where, not only our joy and peace, but our liberty and power in service are forfeited.—Evan H. Hopkins.

Johanna Veenstra, a missionary in Nigeria, was a notable prayer-warrior. She kept alive this thirst for God by obedience to the Spirit. "We need discernment," she said, "but who but the Holy Ghost can impart this? We need courage, to deal with sin before a holy God; and who but the Holy Spirit can give these gifts? How is it that Satan can keep sin hidden in the bosom of the church year after year without our knowledge? Because we lack the wisdom from above to discern it. . . . Most of us are unfaithful, not because we are unconvinced of the need, but because we shirk what is without doubt the most difficult part of our work on the field."

Keep in Sympathy with Heaven

Shall I hide from Abraham that thing which I do? . . . For I know him. . . . And Abraham drew near, and said, Wilt thou . . . not spare the place? . . . And the LORD went his way, as soon as he had left communing with Abraham (Gen. 18:17-33).

The very subtle argument, "You must be with it (society) in order to save it," has oftentimes beguiled earnest men and women to an alliance with the world. The example of Abraham and Lot would seem to show us that Lot, who certainly was "with it," had no power to intercede when the momentous time came. It was Abraham on the lonely hillsides who was the rescuer when the five kings looted Sodom, and it was Abraham whose prayers caused God to "remember Abraham and send Lot out of the midst of the overthrow."—H.

Abraham had never prayed for himself with a tithe of the persistent earnestness with which he prayed for Sodom—a town which was much indebted to him, but towards which, for more reasons than one, a smaller man would have borne a grudge. Lot, on the other hand, much indebted to Sodom, identified indeed with it, one of its leading citizens, connected by marriage with its inhabitants, is in no agony about its destruction, and has indeed but one prayer to offer, and that is, that when all his fellow-townsmen are destroyed, he may be comfortably provided for. While the men he has bargained and feasted with, the men he has made money out of and married his daughters to, are in the agonies of an appalling catastrophe and so near that the smoke of their torment sweeps across his retreat, he is so disengaged from regrets and compassion that he can nicely weigh the comparative comfort and advantage of city and rural life. One would have thought better of the man if he had declined the angelic rescue and resolved to stand by those in death whose society he had so coveted in life.

And it is significant that while the generous, large-hearted, devout pleading of Abraham is in vain, the miserable, timorous, selfish petition of Lot is heard and answered. It would seem as if sometimes God were hopeless of men, and threw to them in contempt the gifts they crave, giving them the poor stations in this life their ambition is set upon, because He sees they have made themselves incapable of enduring hardness, and so quelling their lower nature.

An answered prayer is not always a blessing, sometimes it is a doom: "He sent them meat to the full. . . . But while their meat was yet in their mouths, the wrath of God came upon them, and slew the fattest of them." Probably had Lot felt any inclination to pray for his townsmen he would have seen that for him to do so would be unseemly. His circumstances, his long association with the Sodomites, and his accommodation of himself to their ways, had both eaten the soul out of him and set him on quite a different footing towards God from that occupied by Abraham.

A man cannot on a sudden emergency lift himself out of the circumstances in which he has been rooted, or peel off his character as if it were only skin deep. Abraham had been living an unworldly life, in which intercourse with God was a familiar employment. His prayer was but the seasonable flower of his life, nourished to all its beauty by the habitual nutriment of past years. Lot in his need could only utter a peevish, pitiful, childish cry. He had aimed all his life at being comfortable, he could not now wish anything more than to be comfortable. "Stand out of my sunshine" was all he could say when he held by the hand the plenipotentiary of Heaven, and when the roar of the conflict of moral good and evil was filling his ears—a decent man, a righteous man, but the world had eaten out his heart till he had nothing to keep him in sympathy with Heaven. Such is the state to which men in our society, as in Sodom, are brought by risking their spiritual life to make the most of this world.—Marcus Dods.

God's
Night Shift

There stood by me this night the angel of God (Acts 27:23).

And it came to pass in those days, that he went out into a mountain to pray, and continued all night in prayer to God (Luke 6:12).

The fact of the eminent prayerfulness of Jesus is a lesson for us. The time He chose was admirable. It was the hour of silence, when the crowd would not disturb Him; the time of inaction, when all but Himself had ceased to labor; and the season when slumber made men forget their woes, and cease their application to Him for relief.

The place was well selected. He was alone where none would intrude, where none could observe; thus was He free from Pharisaic ostentation and interruption. The continuance of His pleadings is remarkable. The long watches were not too long, the cold wind did not chill His devotions, the grim darkness did not darken His faith, or loneliness check His importunity. We cannot watch with Him one hour, but He watched for us whole nights.

The occasion for this prayer is notable. It was after His enemies had been enraged, prayer was His refuge and solace; it was before He sent forth the twelve apostles, prayer was the gate of His enterprise, the herald of his new work.—C. H. Spurgeon.

Nights of prayer have been a common practice when God has wrought mightily either in individual lives or in churches. Sometimes God awakened His people in the night because of a particular need.

Livingstone of Shotts tells of the two nights spent by him and his friends in prayer: "I never preached but two sermons that I would care to see in writing. The one was on the Monday after the communion at Shotts; and the other on the Monday after the communion at Holywood; and both these times I had spent the whole night before in

110

conference and prayer with some Christians without any more than ordinary preparation." Livingstone preached that notable sermon he speaks of at Shotts, and over 500 souls were converted to God on that communion Monday.

Mr. Rice, editor of *The Sword of the Lord*, records the blessing which resulted from nights of prayer: "Jacob prayed all night; so did Jesus. Then I would enter into the fullness of prayer life by praying all night. I will never forget the fullness of blessing that came in some nights of prayer in the Galilean Baptist Church in Dallas, and when I prayed until two o'clock in the morning in a Y.M.C.A. at St. Paul, Minnesota, and when I prayed with a great group of the People's Church in Toronto, Canada, led by Oswald J. Smith, in a half night of prayer."

And there is the same pattern running through organizations that experienced the great power of God working on their behalf.

Several members of Jonathan Edwards' church had spent the whole night in prayer before he preached his memorable sermon, "Sinners in the Hands of an Angry God." The Holy Ghost was so mightily poured out, and God so manifest in holiness and majesty during the preaching of that sermon, that the elders threw their arms around the pillars of the church and cried, "Lord, save us, we are slipping down into hell."

Charles Wesley in his journals tells of half nights and whole nights of prayer in which God drew near and he and his associates were empowered to rescue England from paganism and send a revival of pure, aggressive religion over the whole earth.

All-nights of prayer, which afterwards became an important institution of the Salvation Army, were first conducted by Mrs. Booth.

I will try what prayer can do—Lord, give me a measure of that spirit in which Thou didst spend whole nights in prayer.—Mrs. Fletcher.

Fasting to Seek God's Face

As they ministered to the Lord, and fasted, the Holy Ghost said . . . (Acts 13:2).

This kind can come forth by nothing, but by prayer and fasting (Mark 9: 29).

All men who have had spiritual power to prevail with God and man have been men who have learned to sternly deny themselves and keep their bodies under. And as they did this God set their souls on fire and strengthened them with all might in the inner-man to win victories when all odds were against them and thus used them to bless men and nations.

A man should not deny himself food and drink to the injury of his body. But spiritual fasts conducted on Bible lines will bless soul and body when not done to extremes. Any Christian who is willing to forget his body and systematically fast and pray in the interest of his own soul and the souls of others, will reap blessings which will amaze himself and all who know him.—S. L. Brengle.

J. G. Morrison said: "Every great leader who moved his age mightily for God, fasted."

Martin Luther was a weekly faster and God used him to lift the curtain of night that had hung over the world during the "Dark Ages." Luther was criticized for fasting too rigorously, to the probable injury of his health, but his kind of praying moved the world towards God.

John Knox fasted regularly and history tells us that "Bloody Mary," Queen of Scotland, feared his prayers more than the armies of England. Knox prevailed with God through the violence of his determined praying and saved Scotland from Catholicism.

Charles Spurgeon, who knew much of God's blessing, witnesses to the salutary effects of fasting at the Tabernacle: "Our seasons of fasting and prayer at the Tabernacle have been high days indeed; never has Heaven-gate stood wider; never have our hearts been nearer the central glory. I look forward to our month of special devotion, as mariners reckon upon reaching land. Even if our public work were laid aside to give us space for special prayer, it might be a great gain to our churches."

John Wesley tells how fasting was observed by early Methodists with most gratifying effects: "There is something remarkable in the manner wherein God revived His work in these parts. A few months ago the generality of people in this circuit were exceeding lifeless. Samuel Meggot, perceiving this, advised the society at Barnard Castle to observe every Friday with fasting and prayer. The very first Friday they met together God broke in upon them in a wonderful manner; and His work has been increasing among them ever since. The neighboring societies heard of this, agreed to follow the same rule, and soon experienced the same blessing. Is not the neglect of this plain duty (I mean, fasting, ranked by our Lord with almsgiving and prayer) one general occasion of deadness among Christians? Can anyone willingly neglect it, and be guiltless?"

Charles G. Finney, lecturer, writer and evangelist, reveals the secret of his continued power: "Sometimes I would find myself, in a great measure, empty of this power, I would go and visit, and find that I made no saving impression. I would exhort and pray, with the same result. I would then set apart a day for private fasting and prayer, fearing that this power had departed from me, and would inquire anxiously after the reason of this apparent emptiness. After humbling myself, and crying out for help, the power would return upon me with all its freshness. This has been the experience of my life."

Prayer is reaching out after the unseen; fasting is letting go of all that is seen and temporal. Fasting helps express, deepen, confirm the resolution—that we are ready to sacrifice anything, even ourselves to attain what we seek for the kingdom of God.—Andrew Murray.

Persistent Prayer Prevails

The effectual fervent prayer of a righteous man availeth much (James 5:16).

It has always seemed to me that this is one of the strongest texts in the New Testament Scriptures. Certainly I know of no more emphatic statement regarding prayer. It means that prayer that is dead in earnest avails much; the prayer that is offered when men forget to eat and to sleep avails much; it means the prayer that is offered with an all-consuming passion avails much—the prayer offered as the tears blind your eyes, and which finds you saying, "I will not let Thee go except Thou bless me."—J. Wilbur Chapman.

Fraser, a successful missionary among the Lisu tribe, reminds us of his secret: "The opposition will not be overcome by reasoning or by pleading, but by (chiefly) steady, persistent prayer. The **men** need not be dealt with (it is a heart-breaking job, trying to deal with a Lisu—possessed by a spirit of fear) but the powers of darkness need to be fought. I am now setting my face like a flint: if the work seems to fail, then **pray**; if services, etc., fall flat, then **pray still more**; if months slip by with little or no result, then pray still **more and get others to help you."**

Pastor Hsi, a Chinese evangelist used mightily of God, puts us to shame by his earnest entreaties. He records: "On account of many onslaughts of Satan, my wife and I for the space of three years seldom put off our clothing to go to sleep, in order that we might be the more ready to watch and pray. Sometimes in a solitary place, I spent whole nights in prayer, and the Holy Spirit descended. Frequently my mother noticed a light in our bedroom toward midnight, by which she knew that we were still waiting before our Heavenly Father.

"We had always endeavored in our thoughts, words, and actions to be well pleasing to the Lord, but now we realized more than ever our own weakness—that we were indeed nothing, and that only in seeking to do God's will, whether in working or resting, whether in peace or peril, in abundance or in want, everywhere and at all times relying on the Holy Spirit, we might accomplish the work the Lord has appointed us to do. If we had good success, we gave all the glory to our Heavenly Father; if bad success, we took all the blame ourselves. This was the attitude of our hearts continually."

I will not give sleep to mine eyes, or slumber to mine eyelids, Until . . . (Psa. 132:4,5).

> O for the power of wrestling prayer,
>   That pleads, and cannot plead in vain;
> That doth its argument prepare,
>   And, oft refused, returns again,
> "O, bless me, and Thy mercy show!
> Bless, or I will not let Thee go!"
>   —Rev. Thomas Raffles.

"Continuing instant in prayer" (Rom. 12:12). The Greek is a metaphor taken from hunting dogs that never give over the game till they have their prey.—Thomas Brooks.

Importunate prayer surmounts or removes all obstacles, overcomes every resisting force and gains its ends in the face of invincible hindrances. We can do nothing without prayer. All things can be done by importunate prayer.

Importunity is made up of the ability to hold on, to press on, to wait with unrelaxed and unrelaxable grasp, restless desire, and restful patience. Importunate prayer is not an incident, but the main thing; not a performance, but a passion; not a need but a necessity.

                    —E. M. Bounds.

Just Report for Duty

And whatsoever we ask, we receive of him, because we keep his commandments, and do those things that are pleasing in his sight (1 John 3:22).

A mother heard her young son praying and made this wise suggestion: "Son, don't bother to give God instruction; just report for duty."

Oh, my ministering brethren! Much of our praying is but giving God advice! Our praying is discolored with ambition, either for ourselves or for our denomination. Perish the thought! Our goal must be God alone. It is His honor that is sullied, His blessed Son Who is ignored, His laws broken, His name profaned, His Book forgotten, His house made a circus of social efforts.

Does God ever need more patience with His people than when they are "praying"? We tell Him what to do and how to do it. We pass judgments and make appreciations in our prayers. In short, we do everything except pray. No Bible School can teach us this art. What Bible School has "Prayer" on its curriculum? The most important thing a man can study is the prayer part of the Book. But where is this taught? Let us strip off the last bandage and declare that many of our presidents and teachers do not pray, shed no tears, know no travail. Can they teach what they do not know?

The man who can get believers to praying would, under God, usher in the greatest revival that the world has ever known. There is no fault in God. He is able. God "is able to do . . . according to the power that worketh in us." God's problem today is not Communism, nor yet Romanism, nor Liberalism, nor Modernism. God's problem is—dead fundamentalism.—L. Ravenhill.

"Oh Lord," prayed Harold St. John, "some of Thy people are so simple, and some are so subtle. Grant that those who think they are arranging the world may walk with God."

> At Thy dear feet, once pierced for me
> With cruel nails upon the tree,
> I lay my life for use by Thee;
> Henceforth to know no anxious care.
> With cheerful heart my load to bear,
> My sole resort—believing prayer.
> No worry, lest my work be stayed;
> No hurry, lest I be delayed,
> By haste—to prayerlessness betrayed;
> Not careful to be praised of man,
> But only to be taught Thy plan—
> What Thou wilt have me do, I can.
> No greed of gain, for Thou hast said
> That if the beasts and birds are fed,
> Thy children shall not lack for bread.
> How sweet to live alone in Thee,
> In danger to Thy wings to flee,
> The name of Jesus all my plea!
> Before Thee let Thy servant stand,
> To watch Thine eye, Thy beckoning hand
> And promptly move at Thy command.
> So shall my life be one sweet day,
> Lit up by Heaven's cloudless ray,
> A walk with God, a radiant way!
> —A. T. Pierson.

Forty-seven times in the Gospel of John, Jesus said He was under God's orders, and that He never did anything, never said anything, until His Father gave the command. He was listening every moment of the day to His invisible Companion and saying, "Yes." This perfect obedience was what made Him one with His Father and what gave the Father perfect confidence in the Son. It is the reason the Father loves His Son so fondly. This is exactly what the Gospel of John declares that Jesus said over and over and over.—Frank Laubach

Prayer's Place
in Our Plans

In him we live, and move (Acts 17:28).

After he had seen the vision . . . we endeavoured to go . . . assuredly gathering that the Lord had called us (Acts 16:10).

"Get your work from God" is a needed injunction. How often Christian leaders make their own plans, work hard at them, and then earnestly ask God's blessing on them. How much better, as Hudson Taylor felt, to wait on God to know His plans before commencing! Much Christian work seems to have the stamp of the carnal upon it. It may be "good," it may be successful outwardly—but the Shekinah Glory is not there.

The wonderful promise of John 15:7 is prefixed by a far-reaching "if." I wonder if that verse might not be paraphrased: "If you abide NOT in Me and My words abide NOT in you, DO NOT ask whatsoever ye will (for) it shall NOT be done unto you." Perhaps if we examined ourselves more thoroughly before God we might even discover, in some cases, that the whole course of our life was not in accordance with His will. What right would a man have, in such a case, to expect his prayers to be answered? But is not this the fact with regard to much "good Christian work"?

I read a testimony of Dr. Stuart Holden's not long ago, in which he said that one of the greatest blessings of his life had been his unanswered prayers. And I can say the same in my measure. Unanswered prayers have taught me to seek the Lord's will instead of my own. I suppose we have most of us had such experiences. We have prayed and prayed and prayed, and no answer has come. The heavens above us have been as brass. Yea, blessed brass, if it has taught us to sink a little more of this ever-present self of ours into the Cross of Christ. Sometimes our petition has been such a good one to all appearances, but that does not insure it being of God. Many "good desires" proceed from our uncrucified selves.

Scripture and experience certainly agree that those who live nearest to God are the most likely to know His will. We are called to be "filled with the knowledge of his will" (Col. 1:9). The "secret of the Lord is with them that fear him; and he will show them his covenant." We need more holiness, more prayer. We shall not, then, be in so much danger of mistaking His will.

Now all this applies to the prayer of faith. We must have the assurance that we are in the right place, doing the right work. We must be sure that God is leading us, when we enter upon specific prayer. It does not follow that because a thing is the will of God, He will necessarily lead you to pray for it. He may have other burdens for you. We must get our prayers from God, and pray to know His will. It may take time. God was dealing with Hudson Taylor for fifteen years before He laid upon him the burden of definite prayer for the foundation of the China Inland Mission. God is not in a hurry. He cannot do things with us until we are trained and ready for them. We may be certain He has further service, further burdens of faith and prayer to give us when we are ready for them. And He will lead. Abraham would never have been a pattern of faith, if he had remained in Ur of the Chaldees.—J. O. Fraser.

Traversing one night a city street, I was startled by a sharp clanging above my head. On looking up, I found myself directly beneath the tower wherein a huge clock was striking the midnight hour. I took my watch from my pocket, and lo, the slender, overlying hands were pointing exactly to the hour of twelve. It scarcely seemed possible that that tiny piece of mechanism in my hand could keep time with the huge machinery that filled the whole room of the tower; but the proof was before me, and as I gazed at the two pairs of hands of such diverse proportions, I understood as never before that the most insignificant being needed only to be clean, in running order, and divinely regulated, to keep time with divinity itself.—*Christian Observer.*

Preaching
and Prayer

I have preached righteousness in the great congregation: lo, I have not refrained my lips, O LORD, thou knowest. . . . Let all those that seek thee rejoice and be glad in thee . . . thou art my help and my deliverer; make no tarrying, O my God (Psa. 40:9, 16, 17).

Prayer is an essential link in the chain of causes that lead to a revival; as much so as truth is. Some have zealously used truth to convert men, and laid very little stress on prayer. They have preached, and talked, and distributed tracts with great zeal, and then wondered that they had so little success. And the reason was that they forgot to use the other branch of the means, effectual prayer. They overlooked the fact that truth by itself will never produce the effect, without the Spirit of God.

Sometimes it happens that those who are the most engaged in employing truth, are not the most engaged in prayer. This is always unhappy—for unless they, or somebody else, have the spirit of prayer, the truth by itself will do nothing but harden men in impenitence. Probably in the Day of Judgment it will be found that nothing is ever done by the truth, used ever so zealously, unless there is a spirit of prayer somewhere in connection with the presentation of truth.

Others err on the other side. Not that they lay too much stress on prayer. But they overlook the fact that prayer might be offered forever, by itself, and nothing would be done, because sinners are not converted by direct contact of the Holy Ghost, but by the truth, employed as a means. To expect the conversion of sinners by prayer alone, without the employment of truth, is to tempt God.—Charles Finney.

Charles Finney was privileged to have a pleading man, Abel Clary, to intercede for him as he preached. Abel Clary was converted in the same revival effort of which Finney was the firstfruit. "While Finney preached the Word with such logic and power that judges and lawyers, as well as people from all walks of life, were converted by it, Clary remained alone in his room, pleading with God for souls and travailing them to birth.

"A friend said of Abel Clary: 'He prayed nearly all of the time, day and night. Sometimes he cannot stand upon his knees, but will lie prostrate upon his face, and groan and pray in a manner that astonishes me.'

"Finney wrote of him: 'This Mr. Clary continued in Rochester as long as I did. He never, that I could learn, appeared in public but gave himself wholly to prayer.' As a result, Finney's Rochester Revival was one of apostolic proportions and power and one of the greatest in all history."

David Hill, missionary in China, after a period of seeming barrenness said: "It has more than once occurred to me of late that whereas in the commencement of missionary work in any town, great prominence must be given and much time devoted to the public proclamation of the Gospel, yet there may come a time when it is well to go into retirement and spend days alone with God. First 'prophesy upon these bones, and say unto them, O ye dry bones, hear the word of the LORD.' Then, 'prophesy unto the wind . . . and say to the wind, Thus saith the Lord GOD; Come from the four winds, O breath, and breathe upon these slain, that they may live.' This thought has been suggested to me in thinking over the case of Li Mung Chiao, where preaching seems like a drug in the market; where the people seem to count the pearls you offer them a common thing; where after some years of preaching there is not one earnest Christian. At such a place is it not duty to pause, to retire into one's self, to go alone with God, and in confession and penitence, with prayer and supplication and faith, lay the matter before Him? The Lord has certainly a regard for His servants keeping face before those to whom they are sent."

Faith Requires
a Sure Foundation

All the promises of God in him are yea, and in him Amen (2 Cor. 1:20).

Let God be true, but every man a liar (Rom. 3:4).

The Word of God is the foundation for all our prayer, for how could we know how to ask, or for what to ask, had not God so thoughtfully given us His Word with the knowledge of His will unmistakably and clearly portrayed? His promises are the words we take to make our claim. It is little wonder then that Satan should assault the Word and seek to nullify the promises through unbelief.

Vance Havner graphically recounts his struggle: "I started out back in the foothills of the Blue Ridge Mountains. I did not know much. I have not learned a lot since, but I knew precious little in those days. However, I believed the Bible. I just took it and read it as it came. I started in Genesis and was having a great time, taking promises right and left, just like a boy picking apples off a tree in an orchard.

"One day I was met by one of these Bible scholars and was told that those promises were not for me, that they were for the Jew. Well, that discouraged me a little bit, but I said, 'I believe I will give it another try.'

"So I moved over into the New Testament and started down through Matthew, claiming promises right and left. Again I was interrupted and duly notified that those promises were all for the Kingdom Age, not for me. I had never heard of the Kingdom Age before, but since those things were not for me, I did not want to take them.

"So I moved over into the Acts of the Apostles and was daring to claim some, not all, of the blessings that flowed from Pentecost. Once again I was interrupted and told that that was a transitional period, that we were not to press these promises too literally.

"Well, that left me, by and by, with nothing but the Epistles and Revelation, and most of the Revelation was for the future. By the time I had made allowances between groups and marginal references, and tried to look at the Bible through the spectacles of a dozen disagreeing expositors, bless your heart, I was afraid to put down my foot on any verse for fear some scholar would come along like a policeman and order me off private property, and tell me, 'This verse is not for you. Get going, brother, somewhere else.'

"All the promises of God are yea and amen in Christ. Finally, I said, 'Lord, I have heard of a man without a country. If this thing keeps up, I am going to be a preacher without a Bible. If You will give me a verse I can stand on, I will have to have it in a hurry, because they are just about to take it away from me.'

"I got down to that one, 'Let God be true, but every man a liar,' and I have been standing on that one ever since! Brother, I tell you, I believe it is all for me, and I enjoy it.

"We need just that childlike enjoyment of the Word of God. Today we have gotten to the place where people are taking the Bible apart and then they are trying to put it back together, analyzing it, dissecting it—not enjoying it. There needs to be a childlike enjoyment of God's Word and a sweetheart love for Jesus."

Lord Jesus, show Thyself to me
    Within Thy Book divine,
That I may know and worship Thee,
    And draw my life from Thine.
Be Thou the Light of every page,
    The Life in every word;
Through pen of saint and seer and sage
    Reveal Thyself O Lord!

Lord Jesus, show Thyself to me,
    And help me make Thee mine,
That I may walk by faith with Thee
    And prove each word of Thine.
Fulfill Thy promises to me;
    Help me Thy power to claim
Till all my life transformed shall be
    Through Thy redeeming Name!
        —E. Margaret Clarkson.

Prayer Assures
the Oil Flow

The foolish said unto the wise, Give us of your oil; for our lamps are gone out. But the wise answered, saying . . . Go ye rather to them that sell, and buy for yourselves (Matt 25:8, 9).

It is in the nature of flame to burn away the oil by which it is fed. Christian, if you have spent a busy day in God's service and in works of love—if you have stood in the breach, and made a manful protest against worldly sentiments, practices, maxims—if you have run hither and thither on the errand of mercy to the poor, the sick, the dying—if your hands have been busy on some work whereby the truth of God may be maintained and His glory and the interests of His Church subserved: this is all good, so far as it goes, and a subject of devout thankfulness; but still it is external work, and as being external, it necessarily makes a demand upon, and consumes the powers of, the inner life. It is all an outgoing of oil; and if there be no incomings thereof, the flame will not burn long. This good work, this kind work of admonition, this act of beneficence, takes up so much grace—so much grace spends itself in the production of it; and, accordingly, when it has been produced, more grace will be wanted.

Would you know what is the method of nourishing the springs of this hidden life—of securing a reserve of oil? One word understood in a broad and spiritual sense represents the entire method—Prayer. Man of profession, are you a man of prayer? Man of work, are you a man of prayer? Man of activity, are you a man of prayer? If your light is shining before men, are you giving all diligence to have a supply of oil that you may keep it so? And this question carries us beyond the external life altogether into the hidden man of the heart. It leads us away from the flame into the oil-vessels. "Your life (the springs and sources of it) is hid with Christ in God." What of this hidden life? How is it thriving?

The wise virgins had taken pains to lay in a reserve of oil; the foolish ones had taken no such pains. The warning is for those, in whose hearts the flame of the spiritual life has been once kindled.

—E. M. Goulburn.

Unwearied may I this pursue,
    Dauntless to the high prize aspire,
Hourly within my soul renew
    This holy flame, this heavenly fire,
And day and night be all my care
To guard the sacred treasure there.

—Paul Gerhardt.

Henry Craik worked with George Müller at Bethesda Chapel and was very much used of God in the salvation of souls. Andrew Bonar tells of the hidden springs that kept this man's spirit refreshed: "The life of Henry Craik has helped me today in solemn meditation and fasting and prayer. In him I see how the Lord enabled one of His own to go on continually doing all for God, in studying, preaching, writing, keeping him abounding in prayer, and in meditation upon the Word. He was also enabled to live, not before man but God, declining to do many things that might be expected of him, because, if he occupied himself with them, he must neglect retirement, fellowship with God, and family duties."

Seth Rees, evangelist, preacher, and writer, said of his study: "The solitude of this small study is more to my poor soul than all my social intercourse with humanity. It is here that I am transported to the sunlit peaks where eternal verities blaze and glow in unfading splendor, until all that is terrestrial passes into eclipse.

"Amid misunderstandings, peril, toil and pain, an hour with HIM behind these four walls reveals the great white way and lends the strength to climb Heaven's steepest ascents. What strange strength I derive in this solitary nook!

"It is within these sacred walls that I gather strength for a gigantic battle. It is here that I retire for reparation after the battle."

Prayers Outlive an Age

By it he being dead yet speaketh (Heb. 11:4).

Thy prayers and thine alms are come up for a memorial before God (Acts 10:4).

God shapes the world by prayers. Prayers are deathless. The lips that uttered them may have closed in death, the heart that felt them may have ceased to beat, but the prayers outlive the lives of an age, outlive a world. That man is most immortal who has done the most and best praying. They are God's heroes, God's saints, God's servants, God's vicegerents. The prayers of God's saints are the capital stock in Heaven by which Christ carries on His great work on earth. The great throes and mighty convulsions on earth are the results of these prayers. Earth is changed, revolutionized, angels move on more powerful, more rapid wings, and God's policy is shaped as the prayers are more numerous, more efficient. It is true that the mightiest successes that come to God's cause are created and carried on by prayer. God's day of power, the angelic days of activity and power, are when God's church comes into its mightiest inheritance of mightiest faith and mightiest prayer. God's conquering days are when God's saints have given themselves to the mightiest prayer.—E. M. Bounds.

Samuel L. Brengle said: "Some of my prayers I have not yet seen answered, but others that I poured forth with tears and strong desire for His glory and the salvation and sanctification of men fifty years ago are being answered before my eyes."

Lionel Fletcher as a young journalist was amazed at the minister's awe-inspiring words concerning his evangelist guest: "I have never had such a man in my house. I do not know when he sleeps. When I

126

go to his room at night to see if he is comfortable he is in prayer. I saw him go into the church early this morning, and he has not been home for meals."

Lionel Fletcher himself continues the story: "I found the church. I crept in lest I should disturb him. It was in the tropics of Australia. I found him divested of his coat and collar. He lay prostrate at the communion rail. I could hear the agony of his voice and the tears I could see as he pleaded with God for that great gold-mining city that he might lead souls to God. He had been praying all night, and he had fasted and prayed all day. I knelt by his prostrate form and put my hand upon his shoulder and it was wet with sweat. He had never seen me before, but he looked up for a moment and said, 'Brother, pray with me. I cannot live if this town does not turn to God.' He had been there about three weeks without conversions. I knelt by his side. He opened his heart to God and pleaded as I never heard a man plead. I went back to my office awed, humbled, and trembling.

"That night I went to the great meeting and he preached. No one knew he had had no food all day and no sleep at night before the service. He was a great Bible teacher, but not an evangelist, but that night as he preached something happened and the whole place broke under the power of God. That was the first time I had seen a great ingathering of souls."

"Would to God I could always pray with a like ardor," said Luther, "for then I always had this answer, 'Be it unto thee as thou wilt.'"

> It is great to be out where the fight is strong,
> To be where the heaviest troops belong,
> And to fight there for man and God.
> It seams the face and it dries the brain;
> It strains the arm till one's friend is **pain**,
> In the fight for man and God.
> But it's great to be out where the fight is strong,
> To be where the heaviest troops belong,
> And to fight there for man and God.
> —Unknown.

127

Kneeling We Triumph
Volume Two
Compiled by E. F. & L. Harvey
Companion to Volume one. A few titles are: "Waiting, a Proof of our Faith," "Hush My Heart to Listen," "When Prayer is a Cry." Christians from all walks of life are reporting blessings from reading this book. *127 pages*

How They Prayed Series
Volume One—Household Prayers
by E. F. & L. Harvey
This book is a plea for a return of prayer and worship in the home, citing many examples of how praying family members have prevailed with God for their loved ones. Read of parents who prayed for their children, children who prayed for their parents, wives and husbands who prayed for their partners. 19 short, easy-to-read chapters. *119 pages*

Volume Two—Ministers' Prayers
by E. F. & L. Harvey
The first three chapters of this book contain testimonies from various Christians on the benefits of early morning rising for prayer and Bible study. The remaining chapters reveal the emphasis given to prayer in the lives of ministers and preachers from differing denominational backgrounds and nationalities. *104 pages*

Volume Three—Missionaries and Revival
by E. F. & L. Harvey
Read the touching story of Lily Roberts, a missionary in the Congo, who prayed, "Lord, my life for revival," and how God took her at her word. Discover how largely prayer figured in the revival of 1857 and others. Gain an insight into the prayer-lives of various missionaries. *127 pages*

Royal Exchange
Compiled by E. F. & L. Harvey
Thirty-one daily readings which stimulate the reader to exchange his/her weakness for divine strength—an exchange which seems to be the missing dimension of prayer in this busy age. *64 pages*

Asking Father
by E. F. & L. Harvey & Trudy Harvey Tait
A series of short, factual stories which inspire children to approach their Heavenly Father with confidence, knowing that He will honor their prayers. Parents enjoy reading this book as much as their children. It is also an excellent source of material for Sunday Schools. *120 pages*